# God Still Calls

### Joy Kennedy

John Hunt
Publishing Limited

## Dedication

*I would like to dedicate this book to my patient and loving husband Angus, to my two children, Sue and Andrew and to my dear grandchildren.*

Copyright © 2001 John Hunt Publishing Ltd

Text © 2001 Joy Kennedy

ISBN 1 84298 005 X

Designed by Andrew Milne Design

Write to: John Hunt Publishing Ltd, 46A West Street, Alresford, Hampshire SO24 9AU, UK

The rights of Joy Kennedy, author of this work, have been asserted in accordance with the Copyright, Designs and Patents Act 1988.

A CIP catalogue record for this book is available from the British Library.

Printed in Guernsey, Channel Islands

Visit us on the Web at: johnhunt-publishing.com

*Page*

## The birth of this book

Nineteen eighty-one was a disastrous year for me. In January my widowed mother died, and in June my sister died of cancer at the age of only 42, leaving behind two young boys of 9 and 10, to be brought up by their dad alone. In the same month, I was in hospital for surgery and was subsequently told that I would have to have a complete mastectomy. I spent the rest of the year visiting consultants in my home town and also in London. I had also just recovered from being totally housebound with agoraphobia for two years. It was a nightmare and I decided God had forgotten me completely!

My son and daughter coped without me. This was very difficult for my daughter especially and left its mark on her for many years afterwards. My poor husband coped faithfully and ran the household.

One day, when resting and sobbing myself to sleep, I had a dream. It was as if I was being told to write down what I felt. When I awoke I was much calmer and to my surprise, words were coming into my head. I grabbed a pencil and paper and wrote down all that I was hearing. As I read this 'poem' afterwards, I realised it revealed many of my feelings of anger and bitterness...it was horrible really.

For the next year or so, this continued and many of the 'poems' revealed my inner emotions. Then, one day, a beautiful verse emerged, speaking of God's love. This was a surprise, after the others. More words like this were written down and then just as suddenly as they had started, they stopped and I was unable to do it anymore.

Looking back, I believe that much inner healing was the result of this episode and also, the idea of writing became stronger and, ridiculous as it seemed to me at the time, it refused to go away. Believe it or not, I sat on this until 1988! Once again, I was very low and the depression and fatigue which had bothered me all my life on and off, had returned in force. The memories of agoraphobia in the 70s were still reasonably fresh in my mind and the aches of ME lingered and I was very afraid of the present and the future.

Then it happened again…another dream about writing…but what? My life seemed to be a story of hardship, suffering and failure. No-one wanted that! A verse of Scripture popped into my head. It said, "Come to Me, all you who are weary and burdened, and I will give you rest." (Matthew 11:28) This sounded good and I wrote it down. The date was September 9th 1988. Other words came into my mind and I wrote those down too and was surprised when I read them through, because the words were really addressed to me in a very personal way.

Could this be Jesus Himself speaking? (I knew this was possible because it had happened to my maternal grandmother. Also, I was aware of the spiritual gifts of knowledge and prophecy.) It was telling me to take my eyes off myself and on to Jesus. There was instruction here and given in such a loving way! I was quite thrilled. God cared after all. He had not forgotten me. This was even better.

The next morning as I awoke it all happened again, but with a different verse. I couldn't believe it. This pattern continued for a whole year. I wrote down all the verses and something made me keep them safe. I did not keep up the listening for the teaching however. From time to time, over the next few years, I would return to the verses and add what I heard.

In 1998 disaster struck again in a big way! During the last ten years I had actually enjoyed very good health and for the first time ever I had 'lived'. I had moved house twice, now lived in a wonderful part of the country, arranged and enjoyed two weddings, received God's gift of two beautiful grand-daughters, was making the most of retirement and being generally very, very busy with family and Church...too busy in fact and I crashed. Looking back, it was as if God blessed me with ten abundant years and then pinned me down on a bed once more in order to listen to Him more closely. I was suffering from nervous exhaustion and the depression returned in a terrifying way. After several months of rest, the Spring of 1999 arrived and I found comfort sitting in our little summer-house, enjoying the peace and quiet and listening to the sea on some days.

One day, I picked up the verses again, knowing I would benefit. I had just returned from Church and was still thinking about a strange thing that had happened there that morning. I had been trying to sing, but due to the unshed tears inside me I couldn't. I was in a new Church and I knew no-one. Circumstances had meant a change of spiritual home and I was struggling with having no pastor who knew me, no friends who cared, and a very large congregation. Suddenly it seemed as if God poured His Love over me and into me in a tremendous way. It is impossible to describe. This had happened once before and it was like being wrapped in a baby's soft shawl and cuddled. As I sat in the garden in the afternoon, this sensation was still with me but it now felt like oil being poured over me. (I had been told many years previously that this would happen.)

Looking back, I believe this was God's anointing to finish His book. From this moment, for the following four months, I could not stop writing. The words just tumbled on to the paper as I sat each day in the quiet of my little garden. On August 11th 1999 the work was finished...rather a long time after it was started.

So you see, this small book was written, or as I prefer

to say, 'scribed'. I believe it to be inspired by the Holy Spirit, but as you will realise, all words of knowledge and prophecy can contain a human element. I pray that before you read, you will ask God to illuminate that which He means you to hear. Also, as we are instructed to do by Paul, we should, "weigh carefully what is said". (1 Corinthians 14:29)

"But everyone who prophesies speaks to men for their strengthening, encouragement and comfort." (1 Corinthians 14:3)

My prayer is that all who read these Divinely inspired words will receive all that Paul mentions, but much more than this. I pray that you will deepen your relationship with the Lord Jesus Christ through them and come to a truer understanding of the statement:

## God is Love.

Joy Kennedy

*"And we know that in all things God works for the good of those who love Him, who have been called according to His purpose. For those God foreknew He also predestined to be conformed to the likeness of His Son, that He might be the firstborn among many brothers." Romans 8: 28-29*

| Topic | Pages |
|---|---|

| Topic | Pages |
|---|---|

| Topic | Pages |
|---|---|

Part One

# God the Father

**You are precious and honoured in my sight and...I love you.** *Isaiah 43:4*

In the eyes of your heavenly Father you are a cherished possession – a dearly loved child in the family of God – you are, in fact, so treasured that you are priceless.

You are totally unique – nowhere in the whole world will you find anyone exactly like yourself. You are extremely dear and I hold you close to My heart. You are My beloved child and no-one can take your place.

I have watched you through the years. Yes, I have wept, too. I have drawn you to Myself with the cords of Love that will never be broken – it is an everlasting Love. I have watched you over the years. I have seen all your sorrow and distress. I have looked upon you with compassion and with Love and with mercy.

The heights of Heaven are open to those who call upon Me and seek My face.

I call you again, to come to the mountain of God that you might know once more the touch of My hand upon your life. Come, I say, come, with a deep expectancy within and a heart that is open. Come and stand before Me. Come and dwell within the circle of My Love, for it takes an adequate experience of Love to prepare you for an adequate expression of Love.

Come.

Rise up in faith and come.

**Where can I flee from Your presence?** *Psalm 139:7*

You can never fully grasp that your God is omnipresent and present absolutely everywhere.

I am infinite, the beginning and the end – the Alpha and Omega. I am boundless. No-one and nothing can ever contain Me. I am Sovereign and the God who reigns over all. I made the firmament and put the stars in place. I made the deepest oceans and filled them with living things. I made the honey-bee and built in it such capabilities. I am your Creator. Nothing exists that has not been touched by My divine hand. I love every living thing that I have brought into existence. I am the giver of birth and of life.

I know the smallest detail in the lives of each of my precious children too. If I have taken such care to build such capabilities into a tiny insect, how much more do you think I care for you. I am acquainted with all your ways and your thoughts. I love all that I have created and I love you most of all. Could I ever neglect one of My own children? Could I ever leave them to their own devices when they could be harmed?

No matter what, you have a loving Heavenly Father who will always be with you.

See My hand in everything and safely leave it all in my hands.

I am the One and only true God – the God over all.

**Endure hardship as discipline; God is treating you as sons.**
*Hebrews 12:7*

Do not loving, earthly parents correct, train and even punish their child in order to help them learn what is right? Do they allow their little ones to do what they know will harm them? No, because they love their children.

So it is with you, as I discipline you. It is proof of My Love for you. Ask Me what I am trying to teach you. Discipline is unpleasant but there are different ways of accepting it. You can fall into self-pity, thinking you don't deserve it; you can be angry with Me and even resentful; you can accept it as coming from a loving Father, who wants you to know Him better and be closer to Him.

The choice is yours and it is a hard lesson to learn.

**With my God I can scale a wall.** *Psalm 18:29b*

When you face difficulties, remember this My child, I am able to remove them from you or go through them with you.

Either way I will always hold you fast and protect you, according to My promises. In My care you are never helpless. Knowing this you should be strengthened in your spirit and however hard the task ahead, you should be better equipped to face it, to forge ahead and to tackle it. I am your helper. I am He who stops your feet from slipping. I will never ask you to do anything that is beyond your capabilities when hand in hand with Me. Together we go.

Listen carefully to My voice so that you do only that which I ask of you. It is so easy to get caught up in the rush and bustle of meetings and business to do good that you quickly become exhausted. So never start without consulting Me first.

Then you will be surprised at what we can achieve together – but it must always be together – hand in hand, with eyes open to see and ears unstopped to listen.

## I am gentle and humble in heart, and you will find rest for your souls. *Matthew 11:29b*

My nature is tender and loving. I am kind and I care for you and what happens to you.

So often I see you struggling and weighed down. The load you carry is so heavy and I long to soothe you and lift the burden from you. I have a servant attitude for I am the Servant King…a servant is a helper and I am here to be of use to you. So why do you so often turn away and trudge on – so heavily laden? If you will let Me share your load we can work everything out together. Pass your burdens over to Me. I know you have to make decisions and sometimes you have to act by a certain date, but if we work together and you trust Me, your thoughts on

the matter will be the ones I implant in you. If the
burden is one of caring for one of your fellow men, yes,
you may still be weary and tired but I will refresh and
sustain you. I will enable you to cope. I will give you
strength to keep going.

As you walk this way you will find rest in your spirit,
soul and body. Your mind will be full of My Peace. Your
will will be at one with Mine and you will not be
emotionally drained.

### Yet I am always with You; You hold me by my right hand.
*Psalm 73:23*

I know deep in your heart that you believe I am with
you always and so you can say that you are with Me.
You are My child who knows the presence of Christ goes
everywhere with you, day and night.

As an earthly parent watches over their child, so I
watch over you at all times. I send My angels to be with
you too, sometimes.

Just as a young child clutches his parent with his right
hand and finds security, confidence and safety, so you
will find so much more help and assurance when I hold
you by your right hand. There is a 'knowing' that all will
be well – all will be alright when you sense My Presence
close beside you. You are reassured and even when you
take a wrong turning you know that I am still there and

will not forsake you or leave you to struggle on alone.

I delight to see you trust Me and know Me in this way. Though your courage and strength may fail, you find happiness and hope in the reality of your God.

Continue to get as close to Me as you can.

## Love never fails. It always protects, always trusts, always hopes, always perseveres. *I Corinthians 13:7-8a*

My Love truly never fails, but it is a totally unselfish Love, always directed towards others and away from self. It is sacrificial and giving. This is the Love of God. It is a Love that I alone can instil in you because it expects nothing in return.

Many cannot understand this kind of Love, for it goes against natural human tendencies.

Listen to the leading of the Holy Spirit as He quenches your desires and instincts, thus leaving you free to give My Love to others.

Only as you grow closer to Me and have more of My Love in you, can you give this kind of Love, for it is Divine, not to be confused with 'eros' love and lust which the world knows well.

**God is love.** *1 John 4:16b*

I am Love.

I see you always with the eyes of Love – such depth of Love – such compassion. I put love into action in your life as I watch over you – as I hover and brood over you. I am ever attentive to your needs and to your cries and calls for help. Never will I brush you aside – never will I be too busy to answer you. My Love, My Mercy and Kindness await you each day.

I hold you dear to my heart – the Father heart of God – for you are so precious to Me. I hold you constantly in the palm of My Hand and gaze and gaze upon you – My child – so special. What I have created, is so beautiful and as your gaze is returned, so you absorb more of My radiance, light and love. I cradle you in My arms so tenderly and shield you from harm. You are such a treasure in my heart. I have a fondness and affection for you that is far, far greater than you can ever comprehend.

I see you as you will be – purified in My hands – I love you as you are – whatever you may think about yourself is not in My heart, for there is only delight, as I enjoy our intimacy and devotion to each other.

I am the One and only true God – the God over all.

**God...is faithful.** *1 Corinthians 1:9*

All who have accepted Jesus Christ as their Saviour, their Lord and Master...all who have committed their lives to Him...are saved.

All whom God has called into fellowship with His Son, Jesus Christ, will be considered 'blameless' when Christ comes again.

Never fear, however weak you may feel your faith is, you are guaranteed a place in Heaven with Jesus if you have made this commitment and asked Christ to live in you now.

Believe, trust, adhere to, depend on your Saviour and I will not let you down or change My mind, for I am dependable and you can trust My Word.

I wish everyone to be saved and come to a knowledge of the Truth. I want Christ to dwell in your hearts through faith and to know His Love that surpasses all knowledge, that you may be filled to the measure of all the fullness of God.

So, confess with your mouth that Jesus is Lord and believe in your heart and you will be saved.

**I led them out of Egypt and brought them into the desert.**
*Ezekiel 20:10*

My people rebelled against Me. They angered Me. They would not listen. They were disobedient and went their own way. They would not forsake their wicked ways...BUT I loved them. I did not forsake them as they imagined at times, though they turned away from Me. Yet I looked upon them with compassion and with understanding. My Love for them was overwhelming though My heart wept as I watched their waywardness. I could not abandon them even though they went astray. And so it is with you, for I have called you by name and you are Mine for ever.

**He saved him out of all his troubles.** *Psalm 34:6b*

I hear your cries – though you do not always believe this – My ways are not your ways and neither are My thoughts your thoughts.

Sometimes I choose to actually lift you out of your troubles. Other times, I stand by and accompany you through them, often carrying you for most of the time. Only I know the reason.

It is difficult for you to accept that I do not always remove the troubles from your life.

At such times it is necessary for you to hold fast to the truth of My Word and to My promises for strength, for I will sustain you. I will rescue you, but in My way and it sometimes seems to you that I have gone very, very silent and no longer care. I assure you this is not so.

I want you to realise that you need Me more than anything or anyone else and often, the way for you to recognise this is a hard way.

I do promise great blessings to My people, as you read here, but they may not be showered upon you without any hardship on your part, though this is not always so. So when problems arrive, do not attempt to go through them without My help. Thank Me for being at your side even though you may not feel Me there.

**For the word of the Lord is right and true.** *Psalm 33:4*

I am your God, your Saviour, your Healer, your Deliverer. I am trustworthy and faithful. I speak to you through My Word. As they are My Words, they also are real – they too can be trusted…they are reliable for I always speak the truth and never lie.

You can believe and rely upon every word that comes from the mouth of God. The things that are written are accurate and correct. They are genuine. They are honest. Do not swerve from them to the right or to the left. They are life for you and I ask you to feed on them daily, for they are your spiritual nourishment. They are food for thought. They provide all you will ever need for your

spiritual growth and development. They are a light for
your path for they show you the way I wish you to go.
They are a lamp for your feet and they will guide you
always and lead you into the truth of My ways. Keep My
Words and store up My commands within you. Guard
My teachings always and obey them.

Fix My Words in your heart for ever and let the Word
of Christ dwell in you richly.

**Do not despise the Lord's discipline and do not resent His
rebuke.** *Proverbs 3:11*

My one desire for every child of Mine is that they
learn the difference between good and evil and
that they choose My pathway for their life always – that
is, the way of love, for I am a God of love and I
discipline in this love.

I teach and train you by the power of the Holy Spirit
at work within you, in Love. It is for your good only that
I work this way. I care for you deeply and it is in this
caring, that My concern for you is great. I wish to watch
over your development, your spiritual growth, your
character and to enable you to become more Christ-like
in every way possible. I want you to be strong in the
Lord and to know His mighty Power.

Most times this discipline is painful. I know. To be
corrected is not very pleasant at the time, but those who

have been trained by it will bring forth a harvest of righteousness.

So be not bitter or resentful at My hand working in your life. It happens, because I am your loving Father in Heaven and wish to help you and guide you when you take a wrong turn.

## Do not merely listen to the word...do what it says.
James 1:22

My ways are the true ways for living – they bring health to spirit, soul and body. They bring wholeness to you. When you read about My way of living, you will realise the things of which I speak are life-changing and transforming – changing you into a more Christ-like person – but only when you obey what is written will this occur.

Together we work and so I ask you for your co-operation, so that My loveliness may be seen in all that you do and say and think.

So always act upon what you read and study in My Word and so put it all into practice.

---

Actions always speak louder than words, especially to all unbelievers. Their eyes are often upon My children, especially when life seems to be treating them harshly. They are curious to see how you will react when opposition is on every side.

You are very vulnerable at this time and it is so easy to do or say something which you later regret. So be on your guard at all times, most of all in the midst of trials and when your heart is prone to being troubled. At such times as this, ask for My help to keep your eyes off your circumstances and on to Jesus. Repeat aloud, or silently in your heart – in your spirit – appropriate promises and so hold fast to My Word.

Sing praises to Me, for I never change and I will bring you through in My way and in My time.

As you do this, thank Me that I have brought you through before and will do so again, My Love for you will be revealed to others as they watch.

The more time you spend sitting at the feet of Jesus and gazing into His eyes, the more of Me will be absorbed into you. The beauty and radiance of Jesus will then always be seen by others in your actions of love at home and outside of the home, so let My light shine.

**Because He is at my right hand, I shall not be shaken.**
*Psalm 16:8*

I am your God and I have you continually in My grip. I will always hold fast to you and will never let you go, never forsake you and never abandon you, for this is My promise to each of My children. Surely this knowledge of My presence with you at all times and in all places gives you a feeling of security. You are in My safe keeping. I shield you. I know you are open to all the crises and things that befall unbelievers, but I am there with you.

You are not exempt from trouble, pain, illness or any other everyday situation that upsets you in some way…but I am in it with you and I will always help you according to your needs and My plans for you.

You can rest secure in My Love and protection. There will be challenges in your life. I do not promise to eliminate them, but to accompany you through them. This is in order that you can grow to maturity, spiritually. I stand there beside you, holding your hand tightly, teaching, training and strengthening, always.

You will not drown and go under as you sometimes fear, because of My promises.

**(Nothing) will be able to separate us from the love of God that is in Christ Jesus our Lord.** *Romans 8:39*

God is love. Always dwell on this and come to Me in thanksgiving. Love always conquers. Love never fails.

Christ died for you. He gave His life that you might live. His Love was sacrificial and so proves how great it is. Nothing can ever take this Love away from you. No-one can ever rob you of it. It is yours forever and ever. Yes, all My children will face illness, trials, persecution, difficulties, hardship, imprisonment and some, even death.

Suffering will always be there, but allow it to draw you nearer to Me not away from Me. It enables you to identify with Christ.

No matter where you go; no matter what your situation is; no matter what your circumstances are; if you are a child of Mine, this Love of Mine is for you and will never be removed from you.

Nothing and no-one can come between us.

Hold fast to these truths when all seems dark and you feel lost and alone, wondering where you are going and where your next step should be.

This is truth.

**As I was with Moses, so I will be with you.** *Joshua 1:5b*

I am your God and promise to be a constant companion – coming alongside to help – every day and every night – so what have you to fear? I am with you always even to the ends of the earth.

In your life you will face opposition and even persecution, you will be in many storms, big ones and little ones. These are allowed in order that you see just how much I am prepared to help you – just how mighty is My Power. In them, you are equipped by Me to withstand and come through as a conqueror and to be an overcomer.

I do not intend for you to be crushed and defeated in every challenge that you face. I intend that you should stand tall in My strength, being sustained by Me and come through to the other side.

In these times you can grow much closer to Me, as you learn to depend on Me and lean on Me heavily – or you can turn away because what you face is too hard.

I assure you, it will only be beyond you if you travel without Me, and I do not move away from you, for this is My promise.

**The one who calls you is faithful and He will do it.**
*1 Thessalonians 5:24*

When you answered My call to be My child and follow Christ, you surrendered to Me.

Little by little I see you handing over every part of yourself to be under My authority. This is not at all easy for you, as the temptations in your life are many and the distractions great. There is a multitude of obstructions along the way just waiting to devour you.

However, know this, I am ever there with you, to lead you, to help and to carry you as a lamb upon My shoulder, for I am your shepherd and I do not trail behind you or desert you. No, I go ahead and tend each individual in My flock. I would not expect you ever to journey alone, without Me. This would be far too dangerous with all the pitfalls along the way. I come with you, for I am your guide and companion. This, I promise, never to leave you on your own.

So, take heart, when the path is rough and stony, for I always carry the lame and strengthen the weak.

It is My strength in which you walk and I do not abandon you...ever.

## The word of God is living and active. *Hebrews 4:12*

My Word gives Life. It reveals to you what I expect from My children...the way you should live, speak and move.

My Word sets standards for you. It is food – spiritual food.

It is a sword, the sword of the Spirit, which will protect and arm you for battle. This sword is double-edged and will powerfully destroy the works of the evil one whenever He attacks.

My Word is the breath of God coming upon you, stirring and reviving.

It will support and sustain, whatever befalls you. It is active, in that it works within you as you read and inwardly digest it. It is effective, as you will see, when you stand upon it each day and hold fast to the promises therein.

You will discover just how powerful it is, especially in spiritual warfare.

The Word is Christ Himself and He invites you to accept new life in Him.

Live out God's Word each day, so that others can witness its life-changing properties. Show them how effective it can be.

Allow it to change and transform you.

**Your word is a lamp to my feet and a light for my path.**
*Psalm 119:105*

The Bible, My Word, gives you the secret of avoiding all the pitfalls and minefields of your walk with Me.

It is the truths therein that show you how to steer clear from all the darkness and evil in the world around you. It reveals to you how to protect yourself and arm yourself for battle.

This is the light that shows you the way ahead, but only one step at a time. As your feet move forward, often in trepidation, I know, so My Word points in the direction I would have you go.

**The Lord will watch over your coming and going both now and for evermore.** *Psalm 121:8*

I preserve the way of My children and only allow what I can use to bring good into their lives.

I guard their path and watch over them constantly. I will not let their feet slip. Never will I take My eyes off them for a moment. This is how much I love them.

You are one of My children and I see all that you do. I even know what you think. My care and protection for you is constant. Like a shepherd who guards and tends his sheep, so it is with you, as I shield and look after you each day and when you sleep.

Ask the Holy Spirit to give you an awareness of My Presence with you.

**The eyes of the Lord are on the righteous and His ears are attentive to their cry.** *Psalm 34:15*

I am your God and I love My children.

Each one of you is so precious and as any loving father, so I watch over you constantly.

My eyes are never taken off you for a single second. I tend My flock with eagle-eyes. Nothing escapes Me for I am very concerned for you and all that happens to you. Those who have chosen to follow Me...those who live good lives by their obedience to My Word and their willingness to go My way... are ever guarded by Me. I am vigilant. I observe you at all times – the good times, the sad times, the difficult times.

When you need My help and cry out, I am there instantly, right by your side. I listen for your call and promise to answer.

Does this not cheer you?

Does this not comfort you?

Does this not make you feel safe and secure?

Wherever you go, you will still be in My sight and within earshot. There is nowhere you can hide from Me for I am omnipresent and omniscient and always offer you shelter under My wing.

## Taste and see that the Lord is good. *Psalm 34:8*

I long for you to 'savour' Me, My child. Yes – to savour. I invite you to draw closer and to have in your heart a hunger and thirst for Me and of Me – more of My blessings, more of My character, more of My desires – for My will to be your will.

Once you have tried My friendship and My companionship, I feel sure you will want to go deeper into My Love – to have that intimacy with Me that close friends have.

Yes, it is an intimate relationship that I desire to have with you.

Do you not long to know Me better?...to feel My

Presence near?...to experience My Power in your life? So come – I ask you to come – earnestly seek Me; tell Me that I am important to you; that you want more; that you love Me. Make our relationship more personal by 'chatting' to Me – not only in prayer times – all day long, as you go about your business – it does not have to be aloud! Just come and experience My goodness and loving kindness.

Come face to face with Me and soak up My Love, My beauty, My radiance and oh, so much more than you can ever imagine.

### He will not let your foot slip. *Psalm 121:3*

I am here My child, to enable you to walk on your way in confident trust, so that you will not stumble or fall. I am here, to keep your foot from being caught in a trap – I am your confidence – firm and strong. I am here, to make sure you walk uprightly and surely.

I give My angels especial charge over you, to accompany, defend and preserve you in all your ways of obedience and service. They shall bear you up in their hands.

I, the Lord, am your keeper. By day and by night, I guard you and watch over you. I keep you from harm and danger. I guard the feet of My godly ones – those who walk in holiness and righteousness – those who seek to follow Me in love and obedience.

Have no fear of the darkness or of the storms and battles. The evil one can never overpower you so be not afraid. The adversaries of the Lord shall surely be broken to pieces always. My voice shall seem to them like thunder in Heaven and My Power will be made known.

I, who keep Israel, neither slumber nor sleep. My eyes are ever upon you and I am ever watchful.

Take heart, and do not be discouraged when the path is stony and steep and your feet hurt.

**Fear the Lord and shun evil. This will bring health to your body and nourishment to your bones.** *Proverbs 3:7-8*

It is right for you My child, to be filled with awe and wonder as you meditate on Me and My Love – on your God – your Creator.

But I ask to be revered and venerated.

Yes, it is true, I am your close friend and advocate, but I ask you never to forget who I am. Hold Me always in high esteem. Worship and honour Me. Over-familiarity can easily bring contempt and disrespect and soon leads to sin. Beware of conceit, pride, arrogance and perverted and twisted speech.

I am your God – mighty and powerful – He who created the Heavens, the earth and all that is beneath the earth.

**God is love.** *I John 4:16b*

I have wooed you and loved you My precious child, since the day of your conception. I have loved you and drawn you with the cords of Love. I have revealed My heart to you and I have stretched out My arms to you. I have loved you when others have forsaken you and when you have not been able to love yourself – when you thought yourself despised and despicable and rejected. I have loved you and I have wooed you – drawn you so tenderly to My side and into My arms. I have wept over you and reached out to you. For a long time I have sought you. I have sought you down the months and down the years. I have called you and I have loved you with an everlasting Love.

I draw you still with the bonds of Love and bind you to My heart with these cords that can never be broken. Respond, I say, with all your love. Respond with all of your heart.

Dwell in My heart with love and I will heal your wounds with the balm of My Love. I will support and strengthen you. I will keep you and comfort you and you shall be Mine for ever and ever.

Part Two

# God the Son

### Light and life to all He brings. *Carol*
*Hark! The Herald Angels Sing* (Charles Wesley Altd.)

Imagine a picture of a snow scene, the pine boughs blanketed and weighed down. In the background you see a little hut. As darkness approaches, the whole scene is cold, unwelcoming and gloomy.

Then a candle is lit and put in the window. Immediately its glow shines out into the blackness. Its rays send out a warmth into the coldness. The scene is transformed.

When the Christ-child was born in a stable, it was as if a candle-light had been placed in your sin-darkened world. The people who walked in darkness could see a great light which shone upon them and so it is for you today.

For Christ is the True Light which gives light to everyone.

In Him is Life and the Life is the Light of men.

### Glory to the newborn King. *Carol*
*Hark! The Herald Angels Sing* (Charles Wesley Altd.)

When Christ was born, God became a man. Through Him God the Father is revealed – the whole Divine Person and His Nature – we are as one.

Christ is completely human and completely Divine. Yet He did not sin.

The infinite God came down from Heaven to the

depths of the earth.

For a while He laid aside His majesty and His glory –
He did not demand or cling to His rights as God. He
humbled Himself, going so far as to actually die a
criminal's death on a Cross, but He rose again and will
come again.

In His coming the prophecies were fulfilled – so they
will be in His second coming. He will return to earth
and reign.

Bethlehem's babe in the manger will return as
creation's King.

## Come, Lord Jesus. *Revelation 22:20b*

I call you to endure in your faith and look forward to
the hope that I give you and all that I promise which
is yet to come.

The problems and persecutions and all that is evil, I
shall surely bring to an end.

Jesus will return and a transformation will take place.
The earth will be re-created and everlasting Peace will
reign. Evil will be gone forever and you will worship
Me face to face. Paradise will be re-created in the
New Jerusalem.

No matter what happens now, it will end, as I am in
control of all that I created.

There is a wonderful world awaiting all those who

have asked Jesus to be their Saviour and Lord.

No-one knows when this will happen – only Me – but Jesus will come suddenly and unexpectedly so be ready. All will be judged.

## He who comes to me will never go hungry. *John 6:35*

Bread is a staple food. It satisfies physical hunger and sustains your body.

But you are a threefold being; spirit, soul and body and your spiritual side has to be nourished also, in order to prevent you from withering and dying.

Jesus is the bread to satisfy this kind of hunger. Only by a right relationship with Him can spiritual life be sustained.

Invite Him to partner you in your daily walk – at the start of each new day – and you will never starve spiritually. Feed on Him through the Word and by communion with Him in prayer and worship.

## I am the good shepherd. *John 10:11*

A shepherd owns and manages his sheep. He does it because he loves every single one of his flock and knows each one by name. He knows the weak ones, the strong ones, the rebellious ones, and those that have a tendency to wander off and need extra watching and then rescuing. Sheep do not look after themselves. They require never-ending care and attention. They are very fearful and timid, stubborn, difficult and even stupid at times. Each one is ear-marked, literally, so that everyone knows to whom he belongs – life-long ownership, bearing the individual mark of their own shepherd. The shepherd protects and watches over his sheep in all weathers. In the heat of the scorching sun when all is dried up and parched, he provides food and water for them; in the icy cold of winter and in all the storms, he is there; he protects and shields them from their enemies. The little ones or the wounded and tired, he carries across his broad shoulders, holding them safely and firmly.

David, the shepherd king said, "The Lord is my shepherd."

I ask you My child, do you belong fully and completely to the Lord – to Jesus Christ?

Do you trust Him in every area of your life?

Do you respond to His ownership by having a personal relationship with Him?

The Shepherd lays down His life for His sheep, you know.

**I am making everything new.** *Revelation 21:5*

I am your God – the Creator of the Heavens and of the earth.

One day there will be a new Heaven and a new earth.

All that distresses you in these end times, distresses Me also.

One day, when it is right, all will be brought to an end by Me and the Son of God will return in the same manner as that in which He left.

As well as this, you too, as a believer – one who has committed His life to Christ and chosen to live His way – will also rise again with Christ. You will be like Him. You will be with Him forever. You too will be made perfect, like Him who reigns in Heaven with the Father...your sins forgiven, your future guaranteed, to be alive forever, with no more pain and suffering, no more tears, no more sorrow.

Nothing impure will be able to enter the New Jerusalem. Admission will only be granted to those whose names are written in the Lamb's Book of Life. These will escape the lake of fire and permanent separation from God.

I ask you to put your whole trust in Christ and faith in Me and so secure your citizenship in My new creation, that is yet to come.

**God is light; in Him there is no darkness at all.** *1 John 1:5*

I am a holy God, pure and radiant. From Me shines a glorious Light – the glory of God.

My Light pierces the darkness in My children. It reveals all that is not from Me or of Me. It opens up, in

each one of you, that which is hidden and secret –
maybe even hidden from you. All the dross is exposed
and together, as you co-operate with Me, it will be removed.

My Light illuminates the rooms within you that have,
as yet, bolted, barred and closed doors.

My Light calls to you when it shines on the path you
will tread as you follow Me…it is a lamp for your feet,
showing you the next little step on the path of peace.
Walk always in My Light – the Light of My Word – for
this is what it is – cleansing, freshening, purging, setting
apart, and sanctifying, so that you too are holy and
sacred – a true temple in which the living God dwells.

No darkness can remain where I am, for I am the
Light, the Way and the Truth.

Allow Me to shine more into you and break through
all that is not Me. Do not hold fast to that which is not
good.

To shine outwards to others can only happen when
you shine inside first.

So I ask you to open yourself up to the pure,
penetrating Light of God and allow Me to love you into
the person you are created to be.

**Whoever comes to me I will never drive away.** *John 6:37b*

My Father has sent Me to you.
I come to you in His Name, to do His will. I do

not work on My own but with the Father who instructs Me. I can only do what I see My Father doing because whatever He does, I do also. Because of My unity with the Father, I live as He wants Me to live.

This is also true for you, for as you live in union with Me, you too must live as I want you to live, if you wish to honour both Me and My Father.

Those whom the Father gives Me, I will gladly receive and keep with Me for ever. I will never reject them or hurt them in this way. Once they are Mine, they remain Mine forever. No-one can snatch them from Me.

I am here to do the will of My Father and He does not wish Me to lose any of all that He has given Me. He wishes Me to give them new life and raise them up on the last day. He wishes that their names be written in the Book of Life, never to be erased.

**Above all else, guard your heart, for it is the wellspring of life.** *Proverbs 4:23*

Whatever is in the heart overflows into speech, so take great care to ensure that what is in your heart is good, right and pleasing to Me.

In your heart also are your affections and desires. These need to be closely safeguarded too.

I ask you to consider your desires. Are they in line with My Word? Would they delight Me and give Me pleasure? Would they draw you closer to Me or cause a divide, a separation or chasm?

And your affections – to whom do they go? Your feelings of love – am I the first, or the last, or somewhere in the middle? Are they being used to steer you on the right path or are they taking you on a detour and away from Me?

Beware of being side-tracked in all of these areas, for you can so easily be led into sin.

Make sure I am always the source of all that you do.

I am the Way, the Truth and the Life, remember. I am the fountain of life from which you need to drink deeply, in order to be refreshed. I am your reservoir to which you should return again and again.

Then you will grow closer to Me and your desires and affections and love will accord with Mine and you will have true life.

If in doubt, ask yourself, "What would Jesus do?"

**The Lord Himself goes before you.** *Deuteronomy 31:8*

I am a light that gleams brightly in the darkness but only just ahead of you.

I rarely give you the whole scene in one go – it would not be good for you to see such a panorama.

No. I go ahead and lead, but only one step at a time. When I see you following faithfully, I move on a little. It may be necessary to stop for a while and rest in one place.

Think of your journey as travelling on stepping-stones. You would be unlikely to jump ahead too fast. You need you look around and test each step before moving on again.

## Then you will know the truth, and the truth will set you free. John 8:32

The secret of life is revealed in My Word but sadly, many never find the key to unlocking these truths, which give such release and freedom.

For those who have a deep hunger and thirst for more – because they have asked Me for this – to them are given the mysteries of the Kingdom of God.

I need you to dig deeply and frequently into My Word – the Bible. I long for you to make your home there – to live in it – to store it in your heart – to memorise it – to repeat it – to treasure it, for it is rich – to love it and delight in it – to feast on it.

There is power in it that changes and transforms, as new revelation is given to you.

A banquet lies before you – not just crumbs – real meat and real wine. I invite you to come and eat – to be nourished, informed and released in spirit, soul and body, from all that holds you.

Look to the life-giving Holy Spirit to teach you and

give you understanding and enlightenment. Without His help, the words will be lifeless – just words. Do not leave Him out, for it is He who illuminates the Scriptures.

In My Word, through Christ who is the ultimate Truth, the perfect everything, you are clearly shown the way out of darkness and into the light of being the person I created you to be.

This is freedom – not to please yourself, but to die to self and allow Christ to take His place wholly in you.

**The Lord is my shepherd.** *Psalm 23:1*

Meditate on the word 'shepherd'.

What does a shepherd do?

He looks after his flock. He cares for them. He attends to all their needs. He searches for them when they stray and leads them back to the fold. He tends and heals their wounds. He knows each one by name. He knows the fancies, whims and peculiarities of each individual.

This is the care and love an ordinary shepherd shows for his flock.

How much greater is the love and care of the Divine Shepherd for each individual member of His flock. How much more does He want to 'give' to each lamb and sheep in His flock.

You are one of My sheep and I am ever with you.

Watching over you, guiding, leading, helping, so gently and tenderly.

The Lord, truly, is your Shepherd for ever and ever.

## I am making a way in the desert and streams in the wasteland. *Isaiah 43:19b*

Do not despair. Though the tunnel is long and the way is dark I am with you. One day you will see a flicker of light at the end and it will grow and grow until you burst forth. The freshness of dew will be upon you and you will find great happiness, fulfilment and purpose, as My plan for you unfolds. You will be as a rosebud opening up into full bloom.

Those who trust and hope in Me always find the pathway I am making through the desert. Though it seems arid and dry at present, this will not always be so. As you follow My way – the glory road – you will find water. I will quench your thirst with living water. I will always be at your side, loving and caring.

Turn aside from the hurt, grief and sorrow and trust Me to save you, rescue you and lead you into fresh pastures where all is rich and green.

# Part Three

# God the Holy Spirit

**The Spirit helps us in our weakness.** *Romans 8:26*

Did I not promise that I would not leave you comfortless – that you would never ever find yourself alone?

I ascended to Heaven to be with My Father but I have left behind the Holy Spirit. He will guide and teach you all you need to know.

But more than that, when you do not know how to pray or what words to use, He will pray for you. If you but ask, He will intercede for you and help you to pray. He will pray with you in accordance with God's will.

So, as a believer, you are not left alone to handle your difficulties and problems. Even in your prayer time there is help available if you ask. The Father knows what the Spirit says.

When you feel frail and weak – maybe tired out – the Spirit helps you then also. He can speak God's Word into your heart and mind – into your spirit – and so refresh you as He reminds you of God's Promises. Repeat them over and over to yourself for they are food to nourish you in your weakness and at those times when you are struggling.

**The Spirit gives life.** *John 6:63a*

The Holy Spirit teaches you all you will ever need to know about My way of living and what I desire to be in you.

Without the prompting of the Holy Spirit you cannot even see your need for new life, for you cannot see anything wrong with the way you live.

The world at large cannot accept Him.

It is He who convicts you of sin and helps you to understand what sin is – not only the big obvious ones. He is the One who reveals to you My righteousness.

He is the One who guides you into all Truth.

He has been active since the beginning of time when He hovered over the waters.

After Pentecost, He came to live in all those who committed their lives to Christ and so their spirits became united with God's Spirit. This is what gives life – the life of Christ – all that Christ has and is, becomes available to believers at the moment of decision – Christ's Life in you.

Some of you are unaware of the Power of God in the Holy Spirit…some do not know or recognise His 'nudges'.

Realise that this is the voice of God Himself showing you how to become more Christ-like.

This is true life.

**He will guide you into all truth.** *John 16:13*

You have the gift of My Holy Spirit but you do not always recognise Him at work in your life.

I have given Him to you to teach and train you in the truth about Christ and His teachings.

He is there to help you to discern what is from Me and what is false teaching and wrong.

Listen to Him, for there will be much to mislead you in these last days.

My sheep hear My voice. Spend time alone with Me – even in the busyness of your life, you can find Me in the stillness – and you will become more familiar with My voice.

**Not by might nor by power, but by My Spirit, says the Lord.** *Zechariah 4:6*

Just as the lampstand was kept burning by a continuous supply of oil, so it is with My Spirit upon you and within My children.

Only by a constant infilling of the Holy Spirit will you be enabled to succeed in what you attempt for Me. Only by listening to the voice of My Spirit will you indeed know what I am asking of you.

So often what you do in service for Me is to comply with man's needs and desires and, good though your work may be, it is not what I expect of you. So often you become too tired and even exhausted and over-burdened in this way.

So always listen carefully to what I am saying to you. I know each child of Mine well and have plans and purposes for every one. Take time to be still in order to hear My commands rather than man's custom.

The Spirit of God is given to you as you commit your life to Christ.

The Spirit of God is poured out upon you to equip you to carry out My will. He is without measure.

The will of God cannot be accomplished in human strength or by human effort. You will only fail and fall if you move without My Power.

**How much more will your Father in heaven give the Holy Spirit to those who ask Him.** *Luke.11:13*

All good fathers love to give gifts to their children and I am no exception.

I am your Heavenly Father – the perfect Father – one who knows exactly what is right and good for you and what is not.

My gifts to you, My children, are priceless.

The greatest gift you can ever receive from Me is the gift of the Holy Spirit. If you want to be a believer, a disciple, a follower of Christ, and desire to live His way and walk with Him throughout your life on earth, you only have to ask and I will send Him to reside 'in' you. This unites your spirit with the Holy Spirit and you become a son or daughter of God and an heir with Christ in His Kingdom.

The presence of the Holy Spirit within you means you are marked with a seal…My seal…to say that you belong to Me. This is My deposit which guarantees that I will do what I promise to do.

The presence of the Holy Spirit in you proves that you are My child and as such, you inherit eternal life and all the blessings of the Kingdom. His Power transforms you into the likeness of Jesus. He is life-changing and all this is but a foretaste of what is to come.

### That…He may strengthen you with power through His Spirit in your inner being. *Ephesians 3:16*

All My children – My sons and daughters – My heirs to the Kingdom – have the very Presence of God inside them as they make the decision to follow Christ's way of living.

But I want you to know that there is more.

That which I poured upon the disciples at Pentecost is for you also. I give extra power for the tasks I lay before you – an extra outpouring of the Holy Spirit upon you – over you – as well as within you. This is the way in which I equip you for My work.

Often, the work I ask you to do is impossible in your own strength and in your own human efforts.

Yes, the Holy Spirit within, teaches and counsels, but I ask you to come to Me and seek more – much more of Me.

In this way there will be greater boldness, more courage to step out for Me, a deeper closeness and awareness of My Presence.

The Holy Spirit is God Himself and as such, is a very powerful person working for you and with you. Hear My Spirit's voice. Know His Power. To have Him is to have Jesus Himself.

In faith, I suggest you ask for a daily infilling of the Holy Spirit to enable you to go My way.

Appropriate His Power each day and see the difference in your life.

**He breathed on them.** *John 20:22*

To each of My children I give gifts. These are in order for you to witness to unbelievers and to build each other up in the body of believers.

I never ask any of you to do anything on your own or in your own strength. When I call you for a particular task I always equip you to do it.

The power to move in My strength comes from the Holy Spirit living within you, if you have committed your life to Christ.

Sometimes I give you an extra hard task to do and so I give you an extra anointing of the Holy Spirit. To do this, I breathe on you – the very breath of God Himself will be poured out upon you and all over you. You will know the additional power and boldness as it comes upon you and fills you anew. You will sense it – you may even feel it – you will certainly know the difference when you do whatever I have asked of you.

It would be impossible for you to work without this power – you would not stand...you would be drained and weakened if it were not for My strength.

Part Four

# Suffering

**Consider it pure joy...whenever you face trials of many kinds, because you know that the testing of your faith develops perseverance.** *James 1: 2-3*

I know this sounds impossible for you to do, but as you grow and mature in your walk with Me, you will realise why it is actually very easy.

Your life is full of troubles, difficulties, problems, heartbreak, sickness and oh, so many, many 'trials'. I know there are times when you feel like giving up – you don't understand why these unpleasant things are happening in your life and in the lives of those you love and those you hold dear.

"It isn't fair," you say. "Where are you, God? Is this a God of love?"

Nothing makes any sense to you and it's all very tough going. I ask you to stop for a moment and focus on Me instead of the difficulties.

Look back, just for a moment, and recollect what you have already been brought through, although it was hard. Then think of the way your character has changed as you leaned heavily on Me. Do you not ask to have a deeper relationship with Me – for us to be much closer – to love Me more dearly? This all grows in times of trial.

Learn to laugh, to take yourself less seriously – to take a diet of hope and joy.

Pain and problems are inevitable but if you see that in

them and through them, we grow closer and you become
more like Jesus, then you can look upon them as
opportunities for growth, rather than obstacles in your
way. You will be able to see them as opportunities for
Him to demonstrate His grace.

All of this He will help you do if you just ask and in
so doing your trials will become triumphs.

This is how you are able to consider it pure joy in
times of testing.

## (Do not)...lose heart. *Hebrews 12:3b*

You will sometimes feel that the Christian walk is too
hard, far too difficult and even lonely. You may think
I ask too much of you…it can seem like that at times.
You can easily become tired or even exhausted and over-
burdened. This is so discouraging for you.

This usually happens when you have become caught
up in 'business' – more activity than I expect. The
demands and pressures, which the body can put upon
one another, are often enormous. It is not easy to say 'no'
and one becomes unpopular. When you face such
adversity and are over-loaded, remind yourselves of what
it is all about – a relationship between you and Me – a
'getting to know Me deeply' – intimacy with the Father
and the Son through the Holy Spirit.

I urge you, whenever possible, to step aside for a few

moments and be like Mary – sit at the feet of Jesus and gaze in love and awe and wonder – say nothing – silent adoration one to another – I will minister to you without you asking for anything. Enter My stillness for a while, then get up and 'go'.

## I will not forget you. *Isaiah 49:15b*

The children of Israel often felt that I had abandoned them, but it was not so.

You see, it is not I who moves.

When you are in troubled circumstances and feel I am not there and am very silent, do not forget Me. It is difficult to trust Me and believe that I have heard your prayers and am answering them when nothing appears to change and you have no answers.

As a loving parent will not forget their child or abandon them, I WILL NOT DO THIS EITHER.

You are My child. REMEMBER THIS.

Just repeat, "Thank-you Father. You are in control and are working in my situation for my good, always."

## He learned obedience from what He suffered.
*Hebrews 5:8*

I know it can be rather hard for My children to obey My commands and be obedient to My calling and to My teaching.

So it was for Jesus. He chose to obey Me for He loved Me and if you love, you obey.

As He made this choice, so He understands that it is not easy and is thus enabled to help you.

But it is a choice that you are asked to make. It is something that is learned…that is acquired and grasped…through experience…and often that experience is an unpleasant one, in that it involves suffering of one kind or another. Sometimes I have to bring My children to a halt and even allow them to be confined to bed, in order to help them be still and listen to My voice.

When things go wrong in your life and you feel hard pressed and up against a brick wall, I urge you to change your "Why?" into, "What are saying to me, Lord?…What am I supposed to do here?…Help me to hear what you are saying and then give me the strength and courage to act upon this."

## It is God who arms me with strength and makes my way perfect. *Psalm 18:32*

Your life is full of obstacles and challenges but never will you stand alone in them. I am constantly beside you to teach and to guide and lead you through them.

Do not see your path as if it goes through a minefield. This will fill you with anxiety and fear and worry.

See it as one with hills, mountains and valleys.

I will help you to climb when necessary or show you how to skirt around these obstructions – these hindrances.

Hazards, risks and difficulties are all part of your walk with Me because they help us to draw closer to each other as you lean on Me heavily.

There are times when it has to be Me in you, walking, because it is too hard for you by yourself or even with the help of others.

These challenging times are times of great spiritual growth, so I cannot exclude them completely. If the road was not rough or slippery at times and if you were not allowed to slip and slither, you would not see My power at work in your life.

This is the way your relationship with Me is deepened and so you grow and mature in your faith.

## Persecuted, but not abandoned. 2 Corinthians 4:9

May the life of Jesus be ever revealed in your bodies. Do not be overcome by death, but allow life to work in you and through you.

This is for your benefit but also for the benefit of others, especially the unbelievers, as they watch you in the way you think, act and speak or react in your everyday living.

None of you can do any of this on your own. Only as you truly 'live in Christ' is this made possible. It is He in you, that enables you to still shine when you are in total darkness and hard-pressed on every side. Only as you literally cling to Jesus and the Word of God – by the skin of your teeth, sometimes, I know – can you keep going.

But it is so that all My might and power will be revealed and that all glory will be given to Me. People will see just how great and awesome is your God. They will watch My unspeakable, unimaginable Love at work. They will see the Love of God in action as He stays by your side and carries you through. The life of Jesus will be revealed. The unsurpassable love of God will be exposed.

Focus, not on the pain and the circumstances, but on the final prize awaiting you in Heaven, your true home.

## He who began a good work in you will carry it on to completion. *Philippians 1:6*

I am aware that so often you find the way hard and difficult and beset with problems, trials and temptations. Remember this, I have chosen you and called you by Name. You are Mine for ever.

For this reason, I am unlikely to abandon or forsake you or leave you alone on the path.

I know you sometimes 'think' I have done this but I am faithful to My promises – I do not go back on My Word. I have My reasons for being silent at times and one day all will be revealed. It is only in this way that I can tell if you are serious about following Me.

Is your commitment genuine?

These desert times are times of great spiritual growth if you choose to 'lean' on your 'silent' God. They are deepening our relationship.

So do not give up and lose heart though the road be tough, stony and mountainous.

The day Christ died and rose again for you, I began to work for you.

Now you have responded, I work in you by the power of the Holy Spirit.

Do not think there is no progress for there is. I will work throughout your lifetime and this will only finish the day we meet face to face.

**Do not be discouraged, for the Lord your God will be with you.** Joshua 1:9

So often I watch you and am sad because you are so disheartened – nothing seems to go right.

"There is so much to remember," you say to Me. "I so easily slip and tumble or slither about."

I know My way seems hard to you.

There are so many disappointments. So many people let you down, or even reject you and you are unable to use the gifts I have given you, in the way you think I am asking, because of such opposition.

I want you to know that I see and understand. I draw even closer, putting My arm around your shoulder, so lovingly, to encourage you to take another step and not give up.

Fix your eyes on your goal – everlasting life with Me – without such hardship and trials.

Each one of you is watched over so carefully and tenderly by Me and when the time is right – the time I have allotted for you on earth – I will lift you out of it all and take you to be with Me.

When the going is so tough, try to spend a little more time with Me. You need say nothing. Just rest in My Love and ask Me to minister to you – you can do this last thing at night, in bed, just before I send you to sleep.

### Struck down, but not destroyed. *2 Corinthians 4:9*

In your life on earth you face many troubles. They are allowed that My Power and My Presence within you and working through you, may be made known and that it may also be seen by others, that they too might come to know Christ.

As a child of Mine – a son, a daughter, an heir – you have a hope before you. Christ has overcome death itself so that you may have eternal life – everlasting life – now and ever after.

One day your difficulties and persecutions will be over.

You will be rewarded for your faith and receive the joy that lasts forever. Suffering will end. Sorrow will flee away.

Know the inner strength that comes from Me. Draw on it.

In Him, your weakness becomes strength.

## Though I walk in the midst of trouble, You preserve my life.
*Psalm 138:7*

Even when you walk in darkness and there is no light anywhere; even when you have no idea where you are going and seem totally lost and abandoned by everyone – even Me; even in the dark valley of sickness and death; even in a dark tunnel or chasm, do not be afraid, for I am there too!

At such times, you wish to 'feel' My Presence really close and sometimes this happens, but usually you have no sense of Me anywhere near you. But, I promise not to forsake you nor leave you alone.

It is very hard for you to believe and trust in an invisible God, isn't it?

You cannot 'feel' My arms around you in a loving embrace, but I am there. You cannot hear My voice and you find prayer difficult or impossible.

Remember, I am interceding on your behalf and so too are other believers.

All I ask you to do at such times is to trust – have

faith in Me – have confidence that I will keep My promises – expect Me to work – pin your hopes on Me and Me alone.

You can depend on Me and when you have been totally stripped of everything and everybody, there is only Me left anyway. This is how it has to be, for when there are others around, your reliance upon Me is not complete or total.

Initially, this is unnerving for you, but if you rest in My Love, you will see My Power as I care for you, meeting your needs and giving you Peace and reassurance.

## Let us not become weary in doing good. *Galations 6:9*

I ask you to remain loyal to Me whatever your circumstances – whatever befalls you – for your reward is in Heaven. There you will receive the crown of life – there awaits you an unending and glorious future.

Let love be your greatest aim. The victory is yours – guaranteed in Christ, who always leads you in triumphal procession.

Be sure, strong and steady, for nothing you do for Me will ever be wasted, though it may seem so in your eyes. Remain steadfast and immovable, always standing firm in Christ.

Often it is so easy to be downhearted when you have

tried hard to please Me in service and no-one seems to appreciate your work or give you any thanks. Do not dwell on this, for all you do should be for Me, the Lord your God. Allow the rewards and blessings to come from Me and do not be upset by others.

I have given gifts to each of My children, to be used for building up My church and for My glory. Sometimes, it appears that you are unable to use these gifts because others block your way. Let this not unsettle you, trouble you or dismay you. Do not give way to frustration, for these things separate us. Nothing will be wasted.

Stay close to Me and I will make a way in areas that will amaze you. I can open closed doors and show you a direction that you would never have discovered on your own or indeed dared to tread.

**You may have had to suffer grief in all kinds of trials. These have come so that your faith...may be proved genuine.**
1 Peter 1:6-7

Many troubles come your way. I know. Often you are tempted to give in to them and allow yourself to be swamped and completely overwhelmed.

I see them in a different light. In them is the rich potential of a strong faith. To have this developed is something very precious indeed – much more precious than gold.

Look upon these experiences as 'faith processing' and of great value to your spiritual growth. If you are willing to do this, I will help you through the Power of the Holy Spirit. You will then be able to rejoice at such times.

There is great potential in the mountains of adversity and affliction that face My children.

I encourage you to look beyond the pressure and stress that they bring, to the spiritual maturity that is the result.

Just as gold has to be passed through the refiner's fire before it can be pure, so it is with you.

The heat in the crucible becomes almost unbearable, doesn't it?

Love that is strong and sure will guarantee that you survive the fervent heat and you will come forth with faith strengthened.

**Consider Him who endured such opposition from sinful men, so that you will not grow weary and lose heart.**
*Hebrews 12:3*

I ask you not to droop and feel sad and tired and depressed and without hope.

Yes, there will always be much opposition for you, but faint not in acting nobly and in doing good. Do not despair or be discouraged when you appear to be up against a brick wall – when all doors slam in your face.

Many of My children will face much opposition and find themselves in very difficult circumstances. It all draws you closer to Me, as you have to lean on Me heavily, because there is no way you are able to cope on your own.

In it all, you learn to persevere and this develops your character and brings spiritual maturity. You learn to be patient and trusting, as you see how I have carried you through each time and will continue to do so.

You do not struggle on your own, so long as you keep your eyes fixed on Jesus and the ultimate goal.

At the appointed season you will reap a harvest of blessing, if you persist in your efforts to win through.

Be resolute and determined – all this with the help of the Holy Spirit, who is able to assist.

**Do not be afraid or discouraged...for the battle is not yours, but God's.** *2 Chronicles 20:15*

My heart grieves when I see you so disheartened and without much hope. I weep when I see you 'trying' so hard to win the daily battles that you find yourself in.

Yes, you will face daily pressures and stresses, daily temptations and daily burdens. I want you to learn to hand them to Me as they come and trust Me to sustain you through them.

Why not write each one down and tuck the list in

your Bible or pin them to a Cross you have drawn? If
you are tempted to take them back, go and look. We
cannot both have them! Then, thank Me that all is in the
hands of the Father and He is working in your
circumstances.

All I ask you to do is leave Me to take charge but I
cannot do this fully while you continue to struggle and
fight.

Ensure you have your protective armour on each day
and night. My Spirit is within you – a Spirit of Love, not
fear – of Peace, not anxiety and worry.

I will help you if you ask. Realise that I am the One
who does the fighting for you. Work within your limits
but draw on My Strength and Power. It will lift you
above your depression and cause you to rise above the
schemes of the devil. It may not look or feel as if you're
on the winning side today, but if you keep resisting and
persevere and draw near to God, I will crush Satan under
your feet as I promise.

**Though He slay me, yet will I hope in Him.** *Job 13:15*

Sometimes it may seem to you as if I am totally
ignoring your problems and difficulties – it's as if I
am not there any more – not listening – not paying any
attention to your prayers and cries for help.

I assure you that this is not so.

God is Love, remember and a God of Love will not send sickness and tragedy upon His children. They come, however – maybe due to the fallen world in which you live – maybe due to a mistake of someone else – maybe because I have allowed Satan to attack you, as in the case of Job.

But know you this, My child, I only allow Satan to go so far and all the time I am watching. He is a defeated enemy after all. He may be the prince of your world but I am Sovereign over all. I will only ever allow Satan to bring upon you what I can use for My glory.

So do not despair. Be as Job and keep trusting Me and My Promises and put your hope in God always. You live in an unfair world but I offer life with Me forever. This is guaranteed if you have accepted Me as Lord of your life, for I am your Saviour and Redeemer and offer you the hope of being in My Presence eternally.

Your present life is but a journey and pilgrimage to a glorious home in Heaven with Me.

**But now I urge you to keep up your courage.** Acts 27:22

In the face of seeming disaster, in the storms of life and when you feel you have made all the wrong decisions or indeed, taken a wrong turning or even, dare I say, fallen into disobedience, I encourage you to take heart.

Turn once again to Me, for I am your Lord and your

God and I will never forsake you at such times. Providing you are willing to go My way and try again with Me, I always forgive and will help and guide you. So I ask you to be determined to continue to walk with Me.

Do not give up or lose heart, I beseech you.

**You will grieve, but your grief will turn to joy.** *John 16:20b*

Life can be very difficult for My children.
I know and I understand too. Never forget this.

The world's values are often just the opposite of My values. This can sometimes make My children feel like fish out of water – like misfits – as if they don't belong. One day you will rejoice though, so at such times do not become too downhearted and sad.

Do not be overwhelmed with sorrow.

Keep your eye on the future glory and on My promises. Press on towards the goal I have set before you, to win the prize that is waiting for you in Heaven – a crown of glory – your citizenship is there.

**Surely He took up our infirmities and carried our sorrows.**
*Isaiah 53:4*

Your suffering is the suffering of a moment only.
Reflect on My suffering at the end of My ministry.

I do understand grief and sorrow you know, so as I allow you to suffer, I am with you.

glory too. It is necessary for you to suffer at times because as you do, so you learn to depend on Me entirely. You persevere and this changes your character, as I want it to be. You learn My ways and our relationship becomes deeper and much more precious.

Learn to suffer in silence, just talking to Me about it and handing everything over to Me. I will carry it for you and lighten your load so that you can remain at peace, knowing in your heart that all is under My control and that I will never allow more than you can bear.

# Part Five

# Sin and Forgiveness

**Search me, O God, and know my heart.** *Psalm 139:23*

This is a prayer I would have you make very frequently
for it is only when you come to Me for cleansing and
forgiveness that you can grow in your walk with Me. It is
only when you are willing to have Me point out that
which I want to change, that I can begin to work.

How will you recognise sin and your weak areas if I
do not reveal them to you through the power of the
Holy Spirit?

I want you to have values to which you hold fast and
values which you will not forsake at any price or in any
situation. I ask you to be always upright and honest. You
will find that I will lead you through situations in your
life which are very hard and very testing. In this way I
bring to the surface that which I want to deal with and
free you from.

Be open to the Holy Spirit and His prompting and
nudges so that together we can work through these areas.

This is character building and this is what I desire
for you.

**Test me and know my anxious thoughts.** *Psalm 139:23*

This is something I long for in My children – that
their love for Me will increase and grow, to the point
where they feel that their awareness of sin is pathetically
small. I long for you to seek Me and the help of the Holy

Spirit, to help you have a new perspective on what sin is, in God's eyes.

I long for you to realise just how much even the smallest sin can separate you from Me. So often you do not recognise the sin within you and unless you seek the help of the Holy Spirit to point it out, there it remains, as fertile soil for more seeds of sin to grow.

Thoughts may seem unharmful but this is not so. Attitudes can often be sinful too.

I do implore you to let Me search your heart and show you your sin.

Only through true and complete repentance can you receive My forgiveness. It sets you free to work and move and live in the power of God, through the forgiveness of Jesus Christ.

Sometimes, only confessing your sin to another person will make it feel true.

Then, there will be an awareness of the full release of the power of God and of His Love inside you. My Love will truly touch your heart.

## If we claim to be without sin, we deceive ourselves.
1 John 1:8

I am a God of Truth and nothing but the Truth. I am an honest and righteous God.

I expect this honesty to be in each of My children too

– being honest with others is vital – but also, being honest with yourself is equally important.

Do not allow the forces of darkness to pull the wool over your eyes and so deceive you. Satan is the father of lies and would like you to follow his example.

It is so easy to have self-deception. For example, you can see prejudices in others but not in yourself – you have convictions! You can say others are conceited but not you – oh, no…you have self-respect! Maybe you accuse someone of vanity if they care about their appearance – and you – you make the most of what God has given you! Touchiness can be changed to sensitivity. Worry and anxiety can be called concern.

Do you see how easy it is to actually fall into the sin of lies and not even recognise that it is happening?

If you say one thing and practice another is it not lying and Pharisaism – dishonesty, being two-faced?

Do not let false goodness take a hold over you for it is sin. Confess, repent and be cleansed and forgiven.

Then you are free to walk in My Light.

### Jesus bent down and started to write...with His finger.
*John 8:6b*

The woman caught in adultery had sinned – she had broken God's Law – she had failed to live an upright life. I'm afraid all My children fail to walk in obedience from time to time.

I knew this would happen, right from the moment that Adam and Eve fell into disobedience and sin.

Jesus came into the world to put this right. His death occurred because He had to carry the burden of all your sin – He too was separated from Me for a moment because this is what sin does. He cried out in deep anguish.

But He rose again and lives today in you. He is no longer dead – He is the True and Living God.

He stooped down before this woman in her failure and He will do the same for you. He will be quick and ready to come down and meet you in your times of failure. He will come between you and your sin and He will write too – not on the ground, but on your heart and this time you will know what He has written – it is the Father's Love.

I saw your need when I sent My Son to you. When there is no-one else and you are at a very low point, feeling the stones being thrown at you, come before Jesus and He will always be there to cover you, cleanse you, forgive you and stand you on your feet again.

This is the depth of His Love.

**Anyone, then, who knows the good he ought to do and doesn't do it, sins.** *James 4:17*

I would like you to spend some time thinking about the things you do not do – all the things you think I might be asking of you, which you do not make time for…the words you feel you should have spoken but did not…the letters you mean to write that never get done.

You see, sin is not only evil deeds and words. There are sins of omission also – sins of 'not doing right' – you could see them as disobeying something I have asked of you.

Sometimes you keep silent over something, instead of speaking the truth when you are aware of it. Always walk in the Spirit and ask Him to develop in you a deeper awareness of these sins.

**Christ Jesus came into the world to save sinners – of whom I am the worst.** *I Timothy 1:15*

I did not send My Son into the world to condemn the world. He did not come to visit you to point out all your flaws and criticise your way of life. Yes, He may teach you what needs to be changed if you wish to walk in His footsteps. He does not turn you away because of your faults. This is not His way. His way is a way of Love.

He looks upon you and sees not what you are but what you can be in His loving care and with the transforming power of the Holy Spirit living in you and working with you. He came to save the world from their sins. He died an horrific death of crucifixion – in your place. He bore your sins – a once-for-all sacrifice of the shedding of blood, for without this there can be no forgiveness and without forgiveness, it is not possible to enter the Kingdom of Heaven. Forgiveness is not possible without repentance from the heart.

Some do not believe in a God of wrath and believe that at the gates of Heaven they will be accepted and allowed to enter, because a God of Love would not turn them away. God is love and no-one who does not have this Love can live with Him eternally. If this was not so, I would ask you why My Son went through what He did – it would have been unnecessary. When the Son of Man comes again in His glory, He will separate the people. Some will go to eternal punishment, but the righteous, who have followed Him, will go to eternal glory. Everyone has sinned and falls short of God's standards.

Part Six

# Emotions

**There is no fear in love.** *I John 4:18*

My child, when you fear something or someone, there is a great dread existing in you. Now this does not come from Me. My Spirit in you is not one of fear, but one of complete and perfect Love. This kind of love, which comes from Me and Me alone, actually drives away fear and expels every trace of terror. It is impossible for fear and love to live together. You have one or the other but not both.

Do you choose fear as opposed to love? Surely, no! You see, you DO have a choice. Although My Spirit is in you, you can and do choose, sometimes, to live in the old sinful nature.

Reject the fear, in the Name of Jesus and receive My Love, which will repel it all.

Ask for more of My perfect Love and give thanks, always praising my Name.

**Do not be anxious about anything.** *Philippians 4:6*

Anxiety and worry are real killers. They drag you down lower and lower until it seems that there is no way out and you are so desperately weary…the effort for any task seems too great. This is a dangerous situation to allow yourself to be in.

I know there are many, many things in your life, indeed in your world, that trouble you, but I have overcome the world and you live in Me, so you too can be a conqueror and a victor. You too can triumph and live in victory always.

Remember what I said about fear...well, the same applies to anxiety and worry.

My command to you needs to be obeyed...in (not 'for') everything give thanks, for I am Lord over everything. Therefore, do not fret! Instead, in every circumstance, come to Me in prayer, with thanksgiving, with definite requests and make your wants known to Me. I will provide all that you need and all that is part of My plan for you. Sometimes it helps to write down that which is bothering you, draw a picture of the Cross at Calvary... thus reminding yourself visually of all that I have done for you and still do...and then, place your paper on the Cross. If the worry returns, say 'NO' to it, because you have placed it on the Cross and therefore I have it and you do not. You have given it to Me, thus allowing Me to take control...we cannot both have the problem and you have placed both the problem and the solution in Divine hands and I will answer in My way and My time.

**For I am the Lord, your God, who takes hold of your right hand and says to you, Do not fear; I will help you.**
*Isaiah 41:13*

We have a loving relationship with each other, My child....for yes, you are My child for I have chosen you and you are Mine for ever. I truly am your God. I am with you always. I am your Father, your Heavenly Father. Just as an earthly parent takes hold of the tiny hand of their little one to help, so I do likewise with you. Be not afraid to take a step grasping My hand tightly. Put out your right hand...seek My help...it will always be there. I neither slumber nor sleep so I am there in the darkest hours of the night when you feel so alone. I assure you of My strength and always My support and assistance. You do not have to do anything alone, though you have a choice. You can live a victorious life and be more than a conqueror as we walk together step by step, hand in hand. All that you need on your journey I willingly provide...if only you would choose to take it more often. My power flows from My hand through to yours as you grasp Me tightly and trust Me, always depending on Me and not on yourself.

Knowing this, can you be afraid for long?

**Love your enemies and pray for those who persecute you.**
*Matthew 5:44*

My way is a way of Love – always. This is contrary to the world. Those who do not believe in Me do not love those who hurt and harm them, do they? I ask you not to give back evil for evil. Do not return like for like or get one's own back. My way is not one of retaliation.

I do not expect you to take the law into your own hands nor to judge people. You must always leave this to Me. By asking you to love and pray for your enemies – that is, those who hurt you and let you down, those who gossip, those who talk behind your back, those who do not allow you to use the gifts I have given you for building up the body – you can overcome evil with good. If you love those whom you would really like to criticise and get even with and if you treat them well and say nothing against them even though they harm you, they will recognise that Jesus is Lord of your life.

Now all this is only possible for those who have truly given their lives to Christ and so live and move and have their being in Him. You cannot do it on your own – it is not humanly possible. He alone can enable you to show love to those for whom you don't feel love.

You can say, "In Christ I can show God's Love to my enemies."

It is Christ's Love within you that you demonstrate –

not your own.

Whoever loves God must also love his brother even if he is an enemy.

## The one who fears is not made perfect in love. *I John 4:18*

My Love for you is perfect and nothing can separate you from the Love of God that is in Christ Jesus your Lord.

I kindle a flame of Love in the hearts of My children so that they, in turn, can love others.

Whenever fear threatens, recall and speak out aloud all the Scriptures you know about My Love. Declare them aloud, for perfect love drives out fear. You do not have to battle with this, for My Love chases it away.

I have given you a spirit of Love, not timidity, so hold fast to the truth of My Word. In this way, My Love in you grows and grows, for God is Love.

## Love each other as I have loved you. *John 15:12*

This is a command from Me to you. If you choose to follow Me it is not an option – you have no choice. It is what I ask of you and expect you to obey.

You are to love each other as I love you and I gave My life for you, remember – the ultimate sacrifice – sacrificial love.

This is the Love I ask you to give – listening, helping,

encouraging and giving. Each time you see a need, try to meet it in love as I meet your needs in love. Then, when you have given all the love you can, give a little more.

It is My Love you see and it never dries up.

**An anxious heart weighs a man down, but a kind word cheers him up.** *Proverbs 12:25*

What you feel in your heart, in your spirit, will show always on your face. A sad face means a broken heart so often. What comes out of your mouth is the overflow from the heart.

Anxiety breaks one to pieces. This is why I command you not to be anxious, but to bring everything that worries you to Me. Talk to Me about your problems and difficulties. Ask Me to help you work out solutions and answers. Trust Me to do this, even though you may have to wait a while. Place your loved ones in My care and let Me work in their lives too, whether they know Me or not.

Do not become heavy-hearted. I know this is extremely hard to obey when all seems to be going wrong in your life and when sickness befalls you.

Be aware of each other's anxiety and give a word of hope, a word of encouragement, when it is needed. This will lighten a load and help someone to get up again and go on their way much more cheerful.

**Be joyful always; pray continually; give thanks in all circumstances.** *I Thessalonians 5:16*

I ask for obedience in these three commands – this is not easy, but when I see your heart is willing and there is in you a desire to do this, I will help you by My Spirit.

Try to stop your prayers, your joy and your thanksgiving from fluctuating according to your continually changing circumstances.

I do not change and it is to Me you pray and give thanks. The joy of My saving Power at work in you does not change either. The joy of My faithfulness to My Promises always remains.

So think on these things for they are always constant. See the work I have already done in your life and the lives of those for whom you pray. Observe again My Creation. These things are evidence of Me at work and are worthy of joy, praise and thanksgiving. When trials lay heavy on you, thank Me that I am in control still, though it may seem to you that I do not care and am not listening any more.

I ask you to choose to do what I ask and you will see everything and everyone in a different light eventually.

**Do not give way to fear.** *I Peter 3:6b*

I do not wish My children to submit to Me out of fear and dread. Neither do I wish them to serve Me with this attitude.

All I ask is that you choose to co-operate with Me in our walk together just because of your love for Me... because you respect and revere Me.

Just as I ask this of you in our relationship, so I also ask it of you in your relationship with others, whether they are My sons and daughters or not.

However, there must be no meeting unbelievers halfway, for nothing must spoil or mar your relationship with your God.

Submit to one another out of reverence for Christ. Depend always on the power of the Holy Spirit to do this.

## The peace of God...will guard your hearts and your minds in Christ Jesus. *Philippians 4:7*

Whenever you are worried or anxious, I implore you to turn your eyes upon Jesus and talk – turn your worry into a prayer.

If you pray every time you worry – if you pray as much as you worry – you will find that I am able to pour My Peace into your minds and into your hearts. A problem shared is a problem halved, after all. I hear you say, "But I have to make a decision, I have to know what to do; I'm not sure how my loved ones will cope; I'm not sure how I will cope if this or that happens".

I know...I understand. By talking to Me, for this is

what prayer really is, you are unloading your mind. This leaves it clear for Me to put My thoughts in its place and so help you to solve your difficulties.

Each time the worry returns, as it often does, repeat one of My Promises of Peace, over and over to yourself, until you find the storm inside you subsiding and a calmness coming over you, as you trust Me to work and you look expectantly for the answers.

### Love one another deeply, from the heart. *1 Peter 1:22b*

I ask you to be Christ-centred in your life instead of self-centred.

In Christ you are equipped to look to the needs of others and away from your own.

Love that is true, sincere and genuine will overflow from the heart.

It is an offering of yourself to your fellow men and women, believers and unbelievers, as I offered Myself as a sacrifice for you.

It demands selfless giving to all those whom I put before you.

This is Christ's Love and it differs from the world's love…it never gives up.

**You will fill me with joy in Your presence, with eternal pleasures at Your right hand.** *Psalm 16:11b*

My joy is everlasting because it is within you. My Presence inside you – this is not fleeting or temporary, like happiness, which can come and go and is based on circumstances.

So establish and build your life on God, not on situations that you find yourself in.

Keep your eyes fixed on Jesus and off yourself – then you will discover true joy. It will still be there in the midst of the storms of life, which rage around you. Christ died and rose again that you might live eternally with Him.

This is real joy and security.

**Out of the overflow of the heart the mouth speaks.**
*Matthew 12:34*

I invite you to allow the Holy Spirit to cleanse and heal you – to transform you by the renewing of your mind. This part of you is a huge control-centre of your being and determines completely what you think and all your actions too.

On the day of judgement you will have to give an account of every careless word you have spoken.

But do not despair of this hard teaching. Just be attentive to the prods of the Holy Spirit as He reveals the

attitudes and motives in you that He wants to change.
He will help you, as you become willing to be different.
He alone can bring about such radical alteration – the
way you see people, circumstances, yourself and your life.
As you allow this to happen – for it will not take place
without your permission and co-operation – so the Love
of God enfolds and fills your heart.

This will mean that the words you speak will be
different. In this way, what the mouth speaks will be
altered. Your words really will reveal the state of your
heart, deep inside you.

**See to it...that no bitter root grows up to cause trouble and
defile many.** Hebrews 12:15

I want you to realise just how dangerous it is to harbour
bitterness.

I know when you have been let down and
disappointed by those whom you thought were friends,
the natural reaction is to be embittered. Beware! Again I
warn you...be on your guard!

Bitterness works alongside jealousy and anger,
bringing arguments and quarrels among My people. It is
so easy for these carnal characteristics to creep into My
body and work among you, like a cancer.

You are human too, but do all you can to quell their
'destructive' work. A bitter root is quickly formed and its

growth is so rapid – disappointment becomes the seed of resentment.

Do not hold fast to grudges over past hurts. Bitterness in the heart will ruin relationships and halt spiritual growth immediately. You become 'dry and infertile soil' in which I cannot work. The door is then open to all kinds of sin and bad leads to worse.

Flee from this kind of living.

Turn to the Holy Spirit for help to heal the wounds that someone has caused. Only He can fill you anew and help you to see the situation with God's eyes and to look at the people with God's Love.

This prevents the seeds of bitterness and resentment from taking root.

**Blessed is the man who fears the Lord, who finds great delight in His commands.** *Psalm 112:1b*

Fear is of the enemy and a great stumbling block to you all...but take heart, there is a way out of fear – it is possible to be fearless and free.

As you trust Me more and more; as you 'fear' Me, that is to say, as you worship and adore me...as you revere Me and humbly bow before Me, you will find your kind of fear gradually diminishes and decreases until it is no longer there.

I ask you to respect Me and to know that I am the

Almighty God who takes care of you always.

Let the dark shadows fade – the things that haunt you in the night, disappear – as My Love in you grows. Even the fear of death itself will subside, for there is no fear in Love – the two cannot cohabit...you have one or the other...you decide which one to have!

The child who holds Me in high esteem and honours Me by walking gladly in obedience to My commands and My ways, is the one who will be truly blessed by Me in ways far beyond their imagination.

There is such security and peace of mind as you live this way.

## Love your enemies and pray for those who persecute you.
*Matthew 5:44*

In human terms this command is impossible to obey, as the natural reaction is to pay back evil for evil – to get your own back.

However, My ways are not the ways of the world.

For this reason, the world cannot obey a command such as this...it is impossible. My way for you is to do to others as you would like them to do to you. Only as My Love increases within you and you begin to realise what I ask of you, can you even 'want' to live this way.

My Holy Spirit at work within you is the One who changes and transforms your mind, your thinking and your attitudes. Because He lives in you, it is He who loves your enemies and makes it possible for you to pray for those who hurt you and mistreat you. You yourself could never do this, but the Christ who lives within you by His Spirit empowers you to forgive and to love with His Love that is inside you.

This is supernatural living.

## Fear not, for I have redeemed you. *Isaiah 43:1*

I have reclaimed you for My own. I have bought you back and you are Mine and I will not let you go.

Christ paid the price for you by His death on the Cross, so lift high the Cross, for therein lies your salvation.

I have called you by name and claimed you for Myself. You are My child – specially chosen – you are very important to Me and I care very much what happens to you each day and each night. You are no longer a captive or a slave to sin. I have ransomed you by paying a price. You are very precious to Me and I love you. I am your father – Abba – nothing can ever overpower you…I am always with you – beside you – assisting and protecting, so do not be afraid for I am here to help you through.

**For God did not give us a spirit of timidity.** *2 Timothy 1:7*

Fear is destructive. It is not My wish for you that you be afraid of anything or anyone.

When others oppose you or intimidate you, I urge you to call on the Power of the Holy Spirit to help you overcome and withstand, so that you are not afraid of what others might say or do to you. With the help of the Holy Spirit living in you, you can be bold.

Fear robs you of what I have given you – a spirit of love. These two cannot both be part of you. Where there is love, My Love, there can be no fear because you trust Me and are confident of My help and Presence with you. My perfect Love drives away fear.

I ask you to repeat to yourself, over and over again, the above promise.

Reject the fear in the name of the Lord Jesus – take authority over it in His Name – and tell it to go, for greater is He that is within you than he that is of the world.

Meditate on My Love. Drink in My Love. Ask Me for more of My Love and it shall be yours.

**Take courage! It is I. Don't be afraid.** *Matthew 14:27*

I am your light and your salvation – I am your refuge and your stronghold. Fear not. I deliver you from all your fears. Put your faith in Me and trust Me – thus, you put your fears to rest.

Fear paralyses you – it is a very powerful emotion. I understand and will develop in you a faith that overcomes fear. I will use your fears to develop greater faith.

You will realise I am always with you – this will bring renewed assurance and comfort.

Draw closer to Me and to My Word.

Sink deeper into My Love because this will force all fears to flee away.

You have put yourself into the hands of an all-wise, all-loving, all-powerful Heavenly Father and so you are able to face any fearful situation with confidence because you are not on your own. All the terrors of the world cannot remove Me from you. You have God as your Father, Christ as your Saviour, and the Holy Spirit as your guide – you have as your constant companion the One who conquers fear. I will guard and keep in perfect and constant peace him whose mind is stayed upon Me.

## Do everything in love. *1 Corinthians 16:14*

God is Love and God lives in you, therefore His Love lives in you too.

For this reason you are able to live a life of love according to the Royal law. On your own this would be impossible.

It is the Christ within you, in whom you live and move and have your being, who enables you to live in kindness and love – even to the unlovely and those who hurt you. You cannot do this on your own but I can.

So remember this when you find it difficult to forgive and forget those who have let you down and caused your wounds.

Love sacrificially, expecting nothing back – the world does not understand agape love. Never do things for self gain in any way.

Love as I love you.

## Do not be afraid, Abram. I am your shield, your very great reward. Genesis 15:1

Just as I promised Abram that I would defend him and reward him for his trust and faithful walk with Me – so it applies to you also, My child.

When you fear what is ahead of you, remember that I have promised to stay with you and walk alongside you, as well as to go before you. I will not desert you in times of difficulty. As we travel along together and your trust in Me is developed and grows, so you will taste of My blessings, for I do reward all those who are willing to persevere and not give up when faced with problems and when the path is steep and rough.

Contemplate again what you have already come through when you had so many moments of grave doubt that you would survive. You have seen Me at work when you were so fearful and did not know what step to take next or even whether you were courageous enough to take any step again.

My Grace is sufficient for you. I will provide all you need for all you are going through.

Sometimes, it takes time to become a reality and you will be tempted to think you might not make it. Satan is a liar and the father of lies.

I do not promise that which I am unable to give.

**Even though I walk through the valley of the shadow of death, I will fear no evil, for You are with me.** *Psalm 23:4*

Valleys and troughs and abysses are dark, deep places that often seem very foreboding. The mountains that rise up on either side are steep, rugged and precipitous. It can be very dark at the bottom and everything is often damp and boggy, where you can get stuck.

But if you lift your eyes above these, to the sky, there will be light, however small. There is always a way out.

It is so tempting to watch your feet as you squelch along and then you miss the path that leads you upward and out, for it is usually well disguised.

You sometimes feel as though you are trapped and there is no escape from your circumstances.

Allow My Light to shine into them by looking up to Me, for I am the way out for you. I reach into your darkness and enable you to walk in the Light even though the circumstances do not always change. Evil may be surrounding you, but I am watching and as long as you come close to Me it cannot overcome you.

I promise to be the way out for you, so that you can stand up under the trials.

Part Seven

# Character

**To this end I labour, struggling with all His energy, which
so powerfully works in me.** *Colossians 1:29*

How often do I watch you struggling and striving,
tired and weary because you have not taken a little
time with Me to ensure that what you are doing is
actually what I want from you at that moment.

Always go forth in My Name and My Power. In your
own strength you can achieve little, but in
Mine...well...what a difference!

Think of the moments when you have come to the
end of the day glowing because it has been so fulfilling.
Often you have taken Me with you, consciously, chatting
silently to Me as you go, asking for help, asking for
strength and of course I give the energy when I can see it
is a real need, for I am your Provider. What joy it brings
to Me when you have learned to draw on My strength
and at the end of the day, My rest and sleep and
refreshing.

Even during the day, My refreshing is there for you to
take. You will surely be amazed at what you are able to
achieve when My strength and energy are used – it never
runs out.

**Set a guard over my mouth, O Lord. Keep watch over the door of my lips.** *Psalm 141:3*

What is in your heart will always overflow from your mouth.

It is so easy, isn't it, to speak first and think afterwards. Words can crush...words can hurt deeply...words can suffocate and stifle OR words can encourage and build up.

As a child of God it is the latter that I wish you to have. But it has to be a desire of yours in order that I help you to bring this about. You cannot do it on your own. Each morning it should be a prayer that I will guard what you speak to others and it needs to be a desire in your heart to strengthen and inspire them, not to weaken their walk with Me.

**I know whom I have believed.** *2 Timothy 1:12*
Hymn: *I Know Not Why God's Wondrous Grace* (D.W.Whittle)

> But I know whom I have believed
> And am persuaded that He is able
> To keep that which I've committed
> Unto him against that day

My servant Paul was in prison when writing this letter. He was facing death, knowing of his impending execution and so he wrote his final message to Timothy. Paul had lost everything it seemed, but not his faith and trust in Christ. He trusted God to use him in spite of circumstances. He gave his concerns to the One he knew and followed and trusted – the One whom he believed would never let him down.

And so it must be for you My child, for you also are a follower of Christ. Trust in your God, especially when your situation looks bleak and hopeless. Give your problems and difficulties to Christ and He will guard you, your faith and all you entrust to Him for the day – yes, one day at a time remember – even that day, moment by moment.

You are secure in the Love and care of Christ. Let Him work in your life. Develop an intimacy with the Saviour by learning about Him in the Bible, expressing your love to Him in prayer and by obeying His Word.

Learn to follow the Spirit's leading in this way and come to know Him.

**They left and found things just as Jesus had told them.**
Luke 22:13

Peter and John obeyed My commands without question. They knew Me and did not doubt that they would find the man carrying the water jar, in spite of the fact that it would have been a most unexpected sight; ordinarily, the women, not the men, went to the well to fetch water. This man would certainly have been easy to spot in the very crowded streets of Jerusalem.

On another occasion, Jesus commanded two disciples to go to a village and untie a colt, which they would find, and bring it to Him. Once again, they obeyed without question.

Obedience is one of the things I ask of My children – obedience without question. You see, love and obedience are bound together. To know God is to love God. To love God is to obey God.

"Whoever has My commands and obeys them, he is the one who loves Me. He who loves Me will be loved by My Father and I too will love him and shew Myself to him. If anyone loves Me he will obey My teaching."

**To this end I labour, struggling with all His energy, which so powerfully works in me.** *Colossians 1:29*

It is My desire to see each of My precious children growing and maturing in Christ.

Paul wanted to see this too and he laboured to bring it about. He knew, just as I wish you to know also, that he could only work wholeheartedly at the tasks I set before him when he looked to Me for strength and energy.

I do not ask you to serve and work in your strength alone. I give you a spirit of power to work in you and through you. Do not forget this. Learn and grow daily as you set about the tasks I lay before you.

Let your motivation be always love – never pride or fear or any self-ambition.

Know always in your heart that it is your God who provides the strength and energy needed – let Him alone be the driving force. Heed the warning I give, that without Christ, one is doomed to eternal separation from God.

Labour as Paul laboured, to give this warning to others.

### After waiting patiently, Abraham received what was promised. *Hebrews 6:15*

My Word is full of promises for those who love Me and are called according to My purpose. Many may seem to you impossible to be realised, but this is not so. I am a faithful God and always do what I say I will do. You may think they are incredible but you can trust Me to keep My Promises. Do not be like Sarah and laugh, thinking what I say is impossible.

Is anything in your life too hard for the Lord to accomplish? Of course not! Is your day with its problems too hard for the Lord your God to deal with? Is the habit you're trying too break too hard for Him? No, indeed.

For I am personally involved in every part of your life – if you wish this to be so. Sometimes people of great faith do have doubts when I seem to expect the impossible.

Your God is committed to fulfil His Promises, so continue to live in obedience. You can trust Me to do all that I say I will do…but in My time, not yours.

So be like Abraham, wait in serenity, calmness and expectant faith – be patient and do not give up hope.

### The Lord will sustain him on his sick-bed. *Psalm 41:3*

There are times in your life when you feel sick and abandoned. It is all part of the fallen world in which you live.

But you are My child and I am here to help you through and to carry you at such times. Often, I do not remove the sickness but I do promise to be close at your side and with you in it. You may or may not feel My Presence. I am with you in all your suffering because I say I will be. I give support and I help you to endure and My Peace is there too – a knowing that I implant in you – that I am in control, though you know not the outcome.

I do comfort and sustain you and use others too, to help Me.

### Be strong and take heart and wait for the Lord. *Psalm 27:14*

Waiting for Me to act is not easy for you, I know and at times you may think I have not even heard your cries. This is not so. It seems as if I do not

understand the emergency of your situation. This implies
that you think I am not in control of your life and don't
care – or maybe that I am being unfair to you and
making your walk with Me too hard.

I do have My reasons for delaying answers, sometimes
for a very long time. In order for Me to teach you, it
sometimes has to be tough going I'm afraid. Maybe it is
time for you to go a little more slowly and be refreshed.
Maybe you need to be renewed in some way or other.

I want you to trust Me always for I do know what I
am doing.

I hear your cry, "Take me deeper Lord. I want to
know you more clearly and love you more dearly."

Well, one of My ways of doing this is to make you
wait longer for your answers!

In these times, seek Me more and spend more time
with Me. Try to ascertain what lesson I wish you to learn.
Keep your hope in Me for I will never let you down.

**A cheerful look brings joy to the heart.** *Proverbs* 15:30

My gift to you is the Holy Spirit and through Him
you have the fruit of the Spirit.

One segment of this fruit is joy – not necessarily
happiness, I say, but joy.

I invite you to come to Me often because there you
will find deep satisfaction. Your spiritual reservoirs will

be constantly replenished and rivers – not trickles – of living water will flow from you. There will be in you a deep sense of wellbeing as you trust Me.

In order to touch the lives of those around you – the parched souls that are everywhere – you need My constant supply. What is in your heart will show as light and sparkle in your eyes. This I have purposed because unbelievers are drawn to you by what they see on your face and in your eyes.

When you walk closely with Me and depend on Me, you will be sustained by an inner joy. Providing you live and walk in the Spirit each day, the fruit of joy will burst forth naturally and your eyes will shine.

Life's circumstances change and go up and down and this means happiness depends on happenings – joy depends on Jesus. What one must see is this joy. It is not affected by good or bad happenings. It is dependent on Me, on God himself, as you need to be.

Desire to have joy in your heart and your face will be radiant to others.

**I waited patiently for the Lord.** *Psalm 40:1a*

David was used to waiting expectantly for My answer to his prayers. When he did, he found that he was lifted out of despair and into hope. His feet were placed back on firm ground. He was no longer struggling in the mud but was lifted up and steadied by Me. He found he was able to sing praises to Me once more, as his heart and spirit welled up with thanksgiving.

Sometimes, it is that I want to see just how long you will continue to trust Me and so I make you wait. In doing so, you lean much more heavily on Me and depend on Me much more than on yourself.

This brings us closer to each other – though you may not be aware of this until the waiting time is over and your answers have arrived.

You may find that you call out to Me and talk to Me more frequently and you may learn to live each day and night with a prayerful attitude – in other words, praying all the time, though not necessarily on your knees, or alone or quiet.

This is good, for our relationship deepens.

### I will strengthen you. *Isaiah 41:10*

I ask My children to represent Me in the world. This is not an easy calling.

I ask you to show My Love and compassion always, every day.

When the world looks at you and the way you live and the way you tackle life's problems and difficulties, I would like them to see Me.

None of what I ask of you is easy, but I never ask you

to do anything on My behalf without equipping you in every way.

I assure you of My strength and refreshing when you grow weary but also My willpower and strength and determination not to give up.

**Where your treasure is, there your heart will be also.**
*Luke 12:34*

I long to be Lord over every area of your life.

Search your heart and your mind. Listen to the voice of the Holy Spirit. Are there parts of you that are still under your control? This I ask of you.

I speak to you of the things that are important to you in your life. I speak to you of your possessions. I speak to you of your time and talents. See if they are all being used to build the Kingdom of God in the lives of others.

Does your money help others?

Beware! These things can sometimes prevent you from being a generous and cheerful giver, not only financially! Do not let anything stop you from loving others or from serving God.

Take a look at yourself from time to time and ensure that you have everything in your life in the right perspective, for it can easily become out of balance and you can discover that the way you use all that I provide needs some attention.

**Man looks at the outward appearance, but the Lord looks at the heart.** *I Samuel 16:7b*

I see what you are like inside. I know your thoughts, your mind, your will.

Physical appearance means nothing to Me. It doesn't reveal what your true worth is or what you are really like. I judge by faith and character, not by appearance.

Only I have the privilege of seeing your inner character – your desires, your willingness to serve and obey Me. You and I are the only ones who know your 'secret' inner being.

I see your true value. I also see what you can be when My transforming Power works in you.

Give thought to your heart – your spirit – let Me change you into My likeness by the power of the Holy Spirit as He teaches and transforms.

So consider the 'inner you' and give it more attention. What is in your heart, your mind, your attitudes, may be hidden from man, but not from God.

**The battle is the Lord's.** *I Samuel 17:47b*

Do not be deterred or discouraged by the negative and destructive attitudes and words of those around you, when it seems as though you are in the front line of the battlefield and about to fall.

With God to fight for you and with you it is

impossible to lose, even though the outcome may not be as you thought it would be.

I fight for those who keep close to Me and try to live by the Spirit and walk in Him. You may make wrong decisions and mistakes, but if I see your willingness to go My way, I remain your commander.

## The joy of the Lord is your strength. *Nehemiah 8:10b*

Do not be grieved or depressed. Let not your heart be troubled, neither let it be afraid.

I give to you the oil of joy for mourning. Know its comfort and its soothing power. Know its healing.

Over all put on the garment of praise. Sing and be glad, for Christ is alive and will come again to rescue you and take you to be with Him. He gives you His Love in all its fullness. His Presence with you always brings comfort and constant companionship along the way.

I understand you cannot often feel His arms around you. You are unable to touch Him or see Him. I know this is very hard for you, but I ask you to believe these things in your heart and in your spirit. Remember you have the mind of Christ, so accept My Word as truth and be thankful.

Trust Me to have My way with you and as you read My Word and sing praises to Me, let gladness fill your soul. Let the joy of your salvation and eternal life fill your whole being, for one day you will be without sorrow and pain and suffering. They will all cease and you will live forever, without these troubles.

As you sing and are joyful, you will find you are strengthened in spirit, soul and body.

### The Lord gives strength to His people. *Psalm 29:11*

Your Lord, your God, is a mighty God. He is a powerful, creative God, but above all He is a tender, loving God, who passes on His Love to all those whom He calls and chooses – to those who hear His voice in the desert, calling them by name – to those who follow His pattern for their lives.

Your life can be full of stormy patches, sometimes very long ones. Your life can have extremely difficult times when the terrain is rough and stony and you keep on falling down and getting hurt. Your life can be, oh, so lonely.

But take heart, I am here to pick you up and carry you. I will give you strength and courage to continue. I am here to comfort and love you and to encourage you to keep going when you become discouraged and lose heart. I am here to steer the boat when the storms are at their worst. I am here to enable you to weather the storms of life.

The same power that raised Christ from the dead is available to each of My children.

So seek Me – seek this kind of Love in action – every time you struggle and fall. When you feel weak and have reached your limits, don't despair, for I wish you to move in My strength, not your own, in all that I ask you to do.

I have no limits!

### Be...patient in affliction. *Romans 12:12*

Affliction will come to those I love, in many, many forms – troubles, distress, suffering of different kinds, pain, misery, hardship, trials and tribulations – a formidable list from your God of Love!

But I do not send any of these to you. I allow the evil one a certain amount of leeway, but I limit his activity.

It is in the storms of life that you learn and draw closer to Me or the opposite happens and you turn away.

You are free to choose – to lean or to flee.

It is within My power to enable you to remain serene, forbearing and long-suffering, if this is what you wish and ask of Me.

I never force My way on to anyone.

### ...the Lord will be your confidence and will keep your foot from being snared. *Proverbs 3:26*

Trust in Me. Have faith in Me. Depend upon Me and My Word, at all times and in all places.

Do not rely upon yourself and your own judgement

but ask for the wisdom which comes only from God.

Put your confidence in Him who created you and loves you. Rely upon Me always.

Move with courage and boldness in the power of My Spirit, for your God is good and His mercy is everlasting. His Love flows because you are His child and He cares for you.

Walk confidently in Me so that you will not dash your foot or stumble. Walk uprightly and in My righteousness and I will protect you from being led astray and from falling into a trap.

Make the Lord your refuge and He will command his angels to watch over you, to accompany you on your path and preserve you in your walk of obedience and service.

I will follow you if you take a wrong turning and take you by your right hand and gently lead you back. I will protect you and shield you always. I will hide you under My wing in the storms of life, so put your trust in Me alone and we will always walk together.

**Live in harmony with one another.** *Romans 12:16*

In your life I ask you to co-operate with all those whom you meet along the way.

This is a hard task but it is My way of Love and brings Peace to those who are obedient to this command.

Aim to work happily together.

This is made possible, as you keep My Peace within yourself. When you feel stirred up inside, frustrated and irritated by others, quietly hand all of this to Me, and the situation which proves difficult or unbearable, and repeat to yourself words of Peace – My Promises of Peace.

In this way you are focusing on Me and not the circumstances or the people.

Keep this up until you are peaceful inside. Then you will be able to hear Me speak into the problems and guide you through.

This does not mean that you constantly 'give in' and become a door-mat! No! – indeed not.

You just stand firm 'in Christ'. What others say and do is not your fault – leave them to Me.

Breathe in My Calmness, My Serenity, My Stillness and My Peace.

At times you will just have to walk away and sometimes you will have to repent of your part in the disharmony.

## Honour God with your body. *I Corinthians 6:20*

The moment you gave your life to Christ He came to reside in you by His Holy Spirit.

You gave your whole self and your body to Me, so it is no longer under your ownership. As you made this commitment, you were saying to Me that you are not enslaved by the desires and habits of your former life – you are a 'new creation', created in Christ Jesus to do good works which I have prepared in advance for you to do.

As I live in you, it is only right that you look after the temple of the Holy Spirit, by adopting My standards in every aspect of your life and so glorify Me.

**Trust in the Lord with all your heart and lean not on your own understanding.** *Proverbs 3:5*

To trust Me, means that you allow Me to work in My time and in My way in your situation and in your life and in the lives of those you love.

This means that you have to 'let go' and leave everything and everyone in My hands and in My loving care.

This does not mean that you stop caring. You just can't do what is needed and so you believe that I will accomplish it instead.

Write a name or a circumstance on a piece of paper and tuck it an appropriate part of the Bible.

Should you be tempted to take back the burden, look at the paper as a reminder that it is all in My hands and thank Me that I am dealing with it.

**The righteous will live by faith.** *Romans 1:17*

It is part of My plan that all men and women shall be saved through Christ and the shedding of blood; I desire that everyone is 'made right' in My sight and by My hand.

This process is started by them taking a step of faith towards Me, as the Holy Spirit convicts them of their sin and their journey is then continued throughout their life, by trusting Me each step of the way.

As My children continue to walk with Me in obedience and faithfulness, with absolute confidence and trust in Me, they walk from death to life – eternal life, everlasting life.

By the grace of God, you are saved in this way.

By the power of the Holy Spirit at work within you, you can be sure of what you hope for and certain of what you cannot see.

So believe and trust in My character and My promises. I will always do what I say I will do, for I am a faithful God.

So wait patiently, until you see the promises materialise before you.

This is faith and I call you to live always with this expectant hope in Me, your God, who will never fail you.

**Blessed is the man who perseveres under trial.** *James 1:12*

One day your difficulties and pain will be ended and you will receive what has been promised.

This is to be your reward – your blessing – eternal life – living with Me in My Kingdom forever. This is for those who have committed their lives to Christ and have continued to be faithful to Him even in the desert times. To those who love and obey Him even when under pressure of different kinds and in the time of trial – to them will come this reward of a life without pain and sorrow and persecution. They will live in a land of Love, where only Love reigns and rules. Nothing and no-one but Love can be with God in Heaven.

**Faith without deeds is useless.** *James 2:20*

True faith will result in a changed character – a transformation by the power of the Holy Spirit.

As you put your trust in Me and open yourself up to Me and listen – as you obey what I tell you – so, little by little, you will find yourself honed, purified and beginning to shine like a precious stone, free from impurities.

The natural outcome of this is not only a changed person, but a changed way of living, which will result in looking always away from yourself to others – the Way of Love – My Way.

**Those who hope in the Lord...will walk and not be faint.**
Isaiah 40:31

Keep your eyes fixed firmly on Jesus Christ who is the incentive for your belief.

He endured death upon a Cross for you. He died in your place – instead of you. When you think of His suffering, it should encourage you when you are in the midst of trials and when persecution waits for you at the door to swallow you up.

To share in His Glory you share in His sufferings. Count this as a privilege.

Put your trust always in Him and especially when you see no answers and are being called to wait. Do so with patience and expectant hope, for He will not let you down – not ever.

It is all too easy to lose heart and give up. Every one of you will get tired at times, but I am here to listen and help.

My Strength is available and I promise to give it to you. It is not just physical strength to overcome weariness. No...it is more – a determination and will to persevere – a mental strength – a purpose – so that you will not be faint-hearted and unenthusiastic...you will not be found faint and unclear in your minds.

**But those who hope in the Lord...will soar on wings like eagles.** *Isaiah 40:31*

Living My way, My child, requires very little effort on your part. It is purely a life of trust and obedience. There are promises in My Word to fit every situation you will ever come across. Search My Words – find them – stand on them. The strength, the energy, whatever you need, will be met by Me.

You will then be like the eagle, strong and rising to great heights, but not by wrestling, struggling, fighting, striving, straining...often in vain...but by gliding on Divine Power as the eagle glides on the thermals. Wings absolutely still, except for a little movement required to change direction.

So it can be with you, when allowing My Spirit to guide and lead. Walk in the Spirit all day and see how easy it is. Let Me do all the hard work. You glide and soar, all the time listening for direction.

Use Divine Power all day, My child. There is nothing it will not overcome. It never fails. It never runs out. It is My gift to you, My child, this and every day. I want so much that you have it.

Let go and let God.

Part Eight

# Healing

**You have set my heart free.** *Psalm 119:32b*

I wept tears of joy on the day that you finally decided to surrender your life to Me – to commit your life into My hands – to give your heart to Jesus Christ and ask Him to come and live in you by His Spirit. He then became your lifelong companion and friend, as you chose to follow in His footsteps.

Before this you were so bound in carnal thinking and in the ways of the world.

As you gave your heart to Jesus, so all the chains that bound you to the sins of the world and its ways were loosed and your heart became free to live My way.

I delight that you chose the way of truth – to set My standards for your life.

**Forgetting what is behind and straining towards what is ahead.** *Philippians 3:13b*

Sometimes it is not actually possible to forget what is behind – it may only be yesterday – there may be deep hurt, grief, and disappointment. Sometimes I do blot out completely such things but often this is not so because I wish to use what has happened to you to help others and bring glory to Me.

Usually, the past has to be left behind and by My grace and Love, I ask you to move on, move forward. Yes, there are failures and mistakes but when left in My

Divine hands, they will be used and so the time you think was wasted in fact was not wasted. I only allow what I can use and if you continue to walk in obedience and love, in My way, on My path, then nothing is wasted at all. Even the mistakes and seeming failures, I can use to teach you My ways in greater depth.

Leave the past to My mercy, the present to My Love and step fearlessly into the future, moment by moment, with Me as your friend and close companion.

Together, we will "press on towards the goal to win the prize for which God has called me heavenwards in Christ Jesus".

## My soul clings to You; Your right hand upholds me.
*Psalm 63:8*

Let your mind dwell on Me and all that I have done for you.

The mind is so powerful; it controls so much of what happens in your body, your will and your emotions. Cling to Me at all times but most of all in the times of weakness and difficulty, when you are most vulnerable. Cling to Me by fixing your thoughts on Me and My Word.

When your thoughts go astray and ramble on, gently silence them in the Name of Jesus and fix them on My Promises instead. This is not as hard as it sounds once you have tried it a few times.

## The mind controlled by the Spirit is life and peace.
*Romans 8:6*

My child I ask you to guard your thought life. Beware of what you allow your mind to dwell on.

There are so many distractions in your life on earth and it is so easy to fix this 'control centre' of your being on things that will lead you astray and cause you to take a wrong turning.

That which your mind chooses to dwell upon will effect your whole being and yes, your physical condition too. What you think about, will either build you up spiritually or drag you down and into the grip of the evil one. If he can fill your mind with his lies – for he is the father of lies – you will have given him a foothold.

You are no longer controlled by the sinful nature once you have asked God to live in you by His Spirit. Each day you must choose to centre your life – your thoughts, your mind – on the truth of God's Word.

This will enable you to handle the difficulties and problems.

Yes, you have a choice.

Stand firm and say 'no' to wrong, destructive thoughts. As you make this decision and hold fast to the truth of My Word, I will help you and you will overcome and conquer.

**Forgetting what is behind.** *Philippians 3:13b*

Do not hold fast to past mistakes and regrets. Do not feel guilty. You are human and will have things you wish you had not done and which even shame you perhaps.

Just focus on the 'now' and look forward to what you can become 'in Christ'.

Walk with Him today and give thanks that you are forgiven, if you have repented of the things the Holy Spirit brings to mind. The slate is wiped clean. I do not remember and I am your God, so why do you go back to them?

Live in 'where you are now' and leave the transforming to Me.

Just press on in the power of the Holy Spirit and do not become discouraged because it all seems so difficult.

**Those who live in accordance with the Spirit have their minds set on what the Spirit desires.** *Romans 8:5b*

My Son died and rose again that you might live – He opened the way to Me. He offers you a way out from your sinful nature by forgiveness.

As you invite Him to live within you by His Spirit, so this same Spirit teaches you My way of living – My desires for you.

So put to death your old way of life when you chose

what you would do with it.

Enter into a new way of living which brings such freedom.

Listen to the guiding of My Holy Spirit and each day choose to centre your thoughts on Me rather than self.

## Forget the former things; do not dwell on the past.
Isaiah 43:18

My child, it will do you no good to 'live' in the past. Some events were good and some were not.

By all means think about all the things through which I have carried you and come to Me with a thankful heart, but it is better to dwell in the present and trust Me and My Providence for the future.

Let My Love fill you each day as you make time to sit at My feet.

I urge you to stop clinging to past happenings; whether they were good or bad, they cannot be changed so let go of them.

As long as you keep glancing backwards on the way, you are more likely to trip up and fall, so your progress is painfully slow and you move forward only a little.

Do not look down either – look up. What has happened, has happened – let go of it and move on.

There can be no 'growth' by dwelling on the 'might have beens'!

Learn from these experiences and see what I have been teaching you and then walk on – upright and tall – walk with Me holding you tightly – cling to Me and My right hand, as we move but one step at a time.

## Be strong and take heart, all you who hope in the Lord.
Psalm 31:24

Be resolute and strong-minded.

So often you allow your mind to take over and 'run away' with your thoughts.

You can resist thinking what you know is not the Truth. Be determined that, together with My help, you will not have destructive thoughts – ones that seek to defeat you – ones that focus on yourself or circumstances instead of on Me.

Your times are in My Hands so believe this.

I love you and care for you always. Hold fast to this hope and be lifted up.

Every situation you find yourself in will be under My control, so remain steadfast and sure in your faith.

## No-one who puts his hand to the plough and looks back is fit for service in the kingdom of God. Luke 9:62

Once you have made the decision to give your life over to Christ and follow His ways, you are no longer free to please yourself, for I ask you to die to self.

You have chosen to let Christ live in you and this means change, for it is His character that begins to take over. He begins to reign in you.

You have given Me permission to begin transforming and refining you.

I do expect full commitment to this.

It will become difficult for you if you try and have a foot in two camps. There will be a distinct 'uncomfortable' feeling and conflict, so do not be half-hearted and so confuse yourself and so lose your Peace.

## Take captive every thought to make it obedient to Christ.
*2 Corinthians 10:5*

My desire for you is that, daily, you become more and more like Me, bearing My hallmarks and characteristics. Feed on My Word, inwardly digest it. Let it become part of your very being. As you read the Word so you gradually come to know Me. As you know Me so you grow a little more like Me.

Eventually your mind is renewed, providing you are willing for this change to take place. When this happens you will find you begin to think as I think.

This is My desire for you. But, so often, the world interferes and interrupts and gets in the way. You find yourself thinking wrong thoughts that lead to mistakes, wrong deeds and sin.

When this occurs it is My wish that you make yourself aware of it happening. So, be open to the Holy Spirit, who convicts – feel the unease and loss of peace within you. Immediately make a conscious effort to change your wrong thoughts into right thoughts – ones that you know would please Me.

This requires constant alertness and effort on your part but the blessings that follow will overwhelm you and you will know such Peace and fulfilment in your life.

## He heals the broken-hearted and binds up their wounds.
*Psalm 147:3*

Your deliverance will only come through constant trust and faith that does not waver.

Believe with all your heart and soul and spirit that I will do what I promise to do, in My time and in My way.

Put your confidence in Me, for what seems impossible to you is easy for Me.

I will comfort you when you feel hopelessly lost and alone and in a wilderness. I will lift you up and restore your soul.

Arise and come to your Father. Do not remain a prodigal son or daughter any longer. I am waiting with open arms to receive you and promise such an embrace and welcome. I am a forgiving God, gracious and compassionate, slow to anger and abounding in Love.

Do not doubt in your heart that I can do this – do not be like a wave of the sea, blown and tossed by the wind. I will bear your pain, grief and sorrow and bring healing to these wounds and to their memories. The scars will remain to act as a reminder of all that I have brought you through, just as My scars still speak of sacrifice and love – scars for us both, speaking of the love we have for each other.

**The truth will set you free.** *John 8:32b*

Freedom…this is what I want My children to have…true freedom which is NOT like the freedom of the world. Carnal freedom means living only for oneself…pleasing oneself…doing what YOU like…saying what you like and it brings devastation and much trouble.

MY freedom comes when exactly the opposite is done …when one dies to self and the big 'I' no longer exists

"But how can this be?" I hear you say.

I tell you the truth, only when an ear of wheat falls to the ground and dies does it produce many seeds.

The truth of My Word, the truth of My Promises, sets you all SO free. If only you will believe this and hold fast to My Word, you will know that as you die to self and trust Me for everything, there will be freedom.

For instance, My strength has no limits, unlike yours;

it will never run out.

So feed on My Word, My Truth and you will see that you lack nothing. There will be such a release when you understand that nothing you face each day depends on you but on Me. I want you to soar like a bird, to glide along with Me taking all the strain.

THIS IS FREEDOM AND THE KEY IS MY WORD...My teaching.

## The truth will set you free. *John 8:32b*

That which is genuine, real and honest, will give you such release...you will wonder and marvel at the change in you, in your life, in your thinking and attitudes and also in the lives of those around you. For as you live in My Truth, so you release those you love to Me that I might work in them also. For when you hold things against them and expect them to change, instead of you yourself, you actually bind them too and I cannot work so easily.

There is such freedom when you know and live in My truth.

"If you hold to My teaching, you are really My disciples," Jesus said to the Jews who had believed in Him.

If you hold fast to My teachings AND live in accordance with them – if you abide in My Word, for My Word is truth, you will know real freedom.

You will know real deliverance from all your fears, the hurtful memories of the past, true liberty to live your lives in My strength and power. All the chains that bind will be broken. You will no longer live as a caged bird with clipped wings. You will soar on wings like eagles, to the heights with Me, completely loosed into life in the Spirit.

# Part Nine

# Spiritual Growth, Warfare and Victory

**Offer yourselves to God, as those who have been brought from death to life.** *Romans 6:13*

The greatest gift to mankind is being remembered at this season – Jesus Christ, born as a babe in a manger – human in every way.

What a gift!

Such Love prompted this present to you. Such grace broke through the darkness of your lives and shone with a glorious light.

The world into which He came was troubled. People were being persecuted and tyrants ruled. Yet He came to bring Peace on earth – possible only if you look for it in Christ. To know God through His Son means to know Peace.

Though the darkness of sin deepens and threatens to swamp the reason for the celebrations, The Star of Bethlehem still shines brightly.

The best gift in the world was presented to you, wrapped, not in bright paper and ribbons and tinsel, but in swaddling clothes in a manger. Surrounding Him were the animals and His parents. He is alive today and beckons and calls everyone to receive the gift of Himself – this being the reason for His birth.

He invites you to a re-birth – a spiritual birth. He offers Himself and all that He is and all that He has, to you. He can do so much more with your life than you can.

Put to death the misdeeds of the body and live –
glorify Him and honour Him with your body – be one
with Him in spirit and strive to grow more like Him in
thought and word and deed, developing eternal values.

Give yourselves totally as a present to the Father, the
Son and the Holy Spirit.

Yield your lives to Him for His glory.

## I am making everything new. *Revelation 21:5*

Draw aside, My child, and spend time with Me. It is
My desire that we deepen our relationship with
each other and I am asking for your co-operation.

You are looking at life as if through frosted glass.
Nothing is clear. Nothing is bright. Nothing has a sharp
outline. Do you see what I am saying? Do you understand?

I want to wipe away the frost for you, so that
everything is visible, as if the sun is shining on it.

Think of your favourite spot in the countryside where
you love to walk and imagine the sky is bright blue and
cloudless. Sunshine lightens the vista before you and you
smile with delight at the sparkle on the water and the
clarity of the birds and trees and flowers.

I am telling you that this is just how I want you to
see your life, as My plan for you unfolds day by day, little
by little. It is only when you really know Me, the one
and only true and living God, that, yes, all things

become new. Even the old and familiar are seen in a new way and you yourself will be amazed at what you can do when moving under the direction of the Spirit.

Let Me transform you. Let Me change your thought patterns and attitudes so that you look at everyone in a new and loving and compassionate way – as I look on you.

## The old has gone, the new has come!
*2 Corinthians 5:17b*

Only when one lives in Me and I in him does this become possible.

My way is the way of Love. This is the Royal Law.

As you learn more about My Love and just how deep and wide it is, you will be quite overwhelmed. This Love will dwell in you and be part of you when you have accepted Me as your Lord and Saviour and committed your life to Me. Then, and only then, will the old nature, the old self die.

You will be a new creation, created in Christ Jesus, for Him and by Him. My nature becomes your nature. My desires become your desires. My way of Love becomes, your way of Love.

This is the new life I promise.

**Do not work for food that spoils, but for food that endures to eternal life, which the Son of Man will give you.**
John 6:27

The body needs nourishment in order to survive but you are threefold – spirit, soul and body. My children need spiritual nutrition also; this is vital.

There is a storehouse of this food in My Word. Here you will find truth in a world that is full of untruth. My Word stands forever – from now to eternity. Feed on it daily.

Ask Me for a hunger and thirst for the Word of God. Desire more and more of it. I am the Bread of Life itself and no-one who feeds from Me can possibly go hungry. Do not allow yourself to be robbed of this daily food. It is necessary, in order for you to grow in wisdom and maturity.

**The Spirit gives life; the flesh counts for nothing. The words I have spoken to you are spirit and they are life.**
John 6:63

I offer you spiritual bread – the Bread of Life – from Heaven itself. This is food that satisfies and fills you up. This is the bread that leads to eternal life.

To eat of my flesh means to accept Christ into your life and become united with Him in Spirit. Let My Life become your life. In doing so, you allow My Holy Spirit to give you spiritual life.

Without the work of the Holy Spirit it is not possible to know new life in Jesus. For the Holy Spirit is the one who guides you into all Truth; He is the one who teaches and trains you in righteousness and holiness.

The fruit of the Spirit is love, joy, peace, patience, kindness, goodness, gentleness, faithfulness and self-control. These are the qualities I long to see in My children.

It is the Holy Spirit that makes it possible for you to grow more like Jesus. This is Life – true Life. Feed on Me and on My words and let the Holy Spirit show you the way I would have you go. Let Him reveal to you the freedom in the Life that I offer you.

For you, My children, are called to be free, that you might serve one another in Love and live by the Holy Spirit.

**I have been crucified with Christ and I no longer live, but Christ lives in me.** *Galatians 2:20*

I look at you as if you have died with Christ, when you commit your life to Me.

He took your sin upon Himself and you are no longer living under condemnation. You have become one with Christ and all that is His becomes available to you also. He is your brother and you share an inheritance in the Kingdom of God. You have chosen to die to your old life and now walk with Christ, in your new nature. This means that the 'old you' no longer lives. You are now, slowly, being transformed into the nature of Christ – little by little – as the Holy Spirit guides and teaches you what He desires. Be open to His leading – His nudges, His whispers – and repent always of sins, daily, as they are pointed out to you by Him. Seek forgiveness and cleansing. Crucify, with His help, all sinful desires, so that you are not hindered in following Christ. This too is a kind of 'dying' with Him. But, just as He was raised, so too are you, into a new way of living, and you are free to grow into His likeness. You are no longer alone, for Christ lives in you by His Spirit. He is your power for living.

## Count yourselves...alive to God in Christ Jesus.
*Romans 6:11b*

I would that you think of yourselves as 'dead to sin'... that you regard your old sinful nature as dead and unresponsive to sin.

You are now joined – united – to Christ – your spirit with His Spirit. This means that you have a choice as to whether you continue to live with your previous sins, motives, desires and goals for your life. I give you a new start, so to speak; you have the chance to come alive in a new way. With the help, teaching and guidance of the

Holy Spirit, you can be changed bit by bit, just a little at a time, throughout the rest of your life on earth. You can live in a new way – a transformed way – with old bad habits put to death. This you cannot do by yourself, but the Holy Spirit is your helper too. He will only change and remove that which you want Him to. He requires willingness from you and to see a desire in your heart to be different – more Christ-like in character.

**Unless a grain of wheat falls to the ground and dies, it remains only a single seed.** *John 12:24*

Listen, My child, look at the wheat in the fields. There are many blades there. See the ears of corn and the many, many grains of wheat on them. To achieve this, one grain had to die…to be buried in the ground. It then took root and grew and produced the ear that you see before you…an ear with many grains.

This I show you, so that you have a picture of the necessary sacrifice of Jesus. He had to die on the Cross in your place – for your sin – instead of you. He paid the penalty for your sin. But He rose again and is 'planted' in you, if you have asked Him to be – thus, many become His followers. He has shown His Power over death. His resurrection proves eternal life.

This He offers to you, so that you too may take root in Him and live His way.

**Be strong in the Lord and in His mighty power.**
*Ephesians 6:10*

My child, you live in a world wrought with sin and evil and Satan and his army of fallen angels will do all within their power to hinder all Christians in their walk with Me. They are vicious, I'm afraid, and never give up on those who follow Christ. They do all they can to defeat the body of Christ – His Church – they ceaselessly aim to turn you away from Me and back to your old life of sin. But never fear, the prince of your world is a defeated enemy. You are assured, always, of victory through the blood of Jesus. He overcame death on the Cross. Never are you alone in this battle, for this is what it is and you are a soldier in Christ's army and like all leaders, He has equipped you with armour, that you must never take off. Each morning and each night I ask you to put this on. Move forward, always depending on God's strength and the power given to you by the Holy Spirit. Withstand all attacks using the Name of Jesus. Remember the blood of the Lamb protects you.

The gates of Hades will not overcome you if you stand firm, for I am Sovereign and I have overcome the world.

**I am the resurrection and the life. He who believes in me will live, even though he dies.** *John 11:25*

I have conquered death as well as sin, for I am Life. I am He that lives for evermore.

If you commit your life to Me and ask Me to live in you by My Spirit, then all that is Mine becomes yours too. Believe in Me and you inherit My riches, but do not be misled by the word 'believe'. It means to put your whole trust in, to adhere to, to hold fast, to be utterly convinced, to have absolute personal reliance on. It is much more than hope, expect, think, or suppose, for in this sense, most people 'believe' in God…that is, that He lived, in Christ. It goes much deeper. To live, you must die to self and allow Me to live in you instead.

THIS is what it means to 'believe' in Me.

**I have come that they might have life, and have it to the full.** *John 10:10*

Jesus, the Son of God, is the One who gives life, true Life – the only One who can ever do this.

As you accept Jesus as Lord and invite Him to take over your life, so the Holy Spirit breathes in you – comes to reside in you.

You are no longer on your own – you are united with Christ in heavenly places. All that He has, you now share with Him. You no longer battle along in your own strength and energy, for you walk together, with Christ, as one. He is there and by the power of the Holy Spirit guides you in all your ways.

It is only His transforming power at work in you that can change attitudes, alter the way you think and set standards for your life.

Only He can soothe and bathe your emotional hurts. Only He can give Love that will never reject.

Only He can give never-ending companionship along the hard and difficult walk in your life on earth and of course, the best is yet to come…living alongside Him in Heaven, where there is no sorrow or pain and hurt.

He offers life eternal, everlasting life.

He offers life on a higher plane on earth too, because of His forgiveness, love and guidance.

Is this life not worth having now and for ever?

## He trains my hands for battle. *2 Samuel 22:35*

As My children, you will find yourselves in a battle, from the moment that you accept Christ as your Lord and Master.

The prince of this world will begin to show an interest in you. Do not let this deter you, for I have overcome the world and I reign supreme. I am Sovereign over all that I have created. I only allow the evil one to do what I can then use for My glory.

I have provided you with armour with which you should clothe yourself each morning and each night. You have been given the belt of truth, the breastplate of righteousness, the shoes of the gospel of peace, the helmet of salvation, the sword of the Spirit and the shield of faith.

Also, you have the Name of Jesus at which every knee shall bow. The blood of Jesus, shed for you, holds great power and destroys the works of the evil one.

Put on a garment of praise too, because the powers of darkness loathe this and I inhabit the praises of My people.

So you are well equipped for spiritual warfare and I urge you not to be intimidated. I watch his every move.

My Love will always protect you from evil forces, for in Christ you are a conqueror.

**Continue to live in Him, rooted and built up in Him.**
*Colossians 2:7*

To all plants and trees I have given roots. They are there in order to give nourishment, which then gives growth and fruit.

And so it is with you. Draw your very life-blood from Christ. He should be the source of your spiritual bread and water – your spiritual food. Be united with him. Be filled with His Love. Feed and drink from Him always. He provides all you need to grow to spiritual maturity. Read and inwardly digest His Word. Obey His commands. Draw sustenance from Him as He directs. Learn from Him and be strengthened and encouraged. May Christ dwell in you so that you are firmly planted in God's Love. Be continually built up in Him who loves you and gave His life for you that you might live.

Let your roots go deep down into the soil of His Love, as you learn to trust Him more and more. Be filled up with God Himself, as you give every part of your being over to His Lordship.

### The letter kills, but the Spirit gives life. *2 Corinthians 3:6b*

I gave My commands to Moses; they were written on tablets of stone and so My Law came into being.

This was the old covenant, but its glory faded into nothing – indeed the face of Moses lost its radiance of the glory of God.

How much greater was My plan, to call My children into a life of obedience to Me.

The old law gave an awareness to My children of their sin, but there had to be a sacrifice in order to receive forgiveness. The whole earth was doomed to die, without the shedding of blood.

Then came My new plan – salvation through Christ. The Son of God Himself became the sacrifice for one and all and through His blood you have eternal life.

Here I give you the opportunity to make yourself

right with God. Under the new promise or agreement –
the new covenant I make with my people – the veil of
misunderstanding is removed. As well as becoming aware
of your uncleanness – your sin – and your need for
forgiveness, by My grace you come to realise the only
path that leads to God is through Christ.

Only by grace can you enter the Kingdom of God
and receive new life through the power of the Holy Spirit.

### Where the Spirit of the Lord is, there is freedom.
*2 Corinthians 3:17b*

No-one is able to enter My Kingdom, the Kingdom
of God, through good works or through being a
good person, for these standards of 'goodness and right
living' are not Mine.

The Holy Spirit is the power of God that removes the
blinkers from your eyes. He shows you that there is no
way you can 'please' God by keeping rules and laws as in
the old covenant and by performing ceremonies as they
did, or by trying to live a good life in your eyes. It is
impossible to satisfy God in this way.

When you commit your life to Christ, and only then,
are your eyes and heart opened up and the veil removed.

Then you can see that you cannot earn a place in
God's Kingdom by just obeying the Ten Commandments
– you see, this is not the way to salvation and it is only

through Christ that you can receive new life. In Him there is a new way of living, free from the burden of guilt and sin, and the weight of having to be worthy of a place in Heaven. The way in is through trusting Christ as your Saviour – it is a way of Love – you are accepted as you are, forgiven, cleansed and freed and live a new and different life in Him who loved you so much that He gave His Life for you.

**I am come that they might have life, and that they might have it more abundantly.** *John 10:10 (KJV)*

The way of living I intend for each child of Mine is vitalising and stimulating. It is fulfilling and gives such freedom. It gives release from all the things that have hurt you, from the many disappointments, failures and mistakes and from the past things that haunt you. It enables you to become the person I intend you to be, with all the guilt removed and your sin-stained past put to death.

This abundant life, or freedom-living, is a gift and it comes to you little by little, as you grow closer to Me and come to know what I offer you. It is a gradual and lifelong process of learning and growing. It is a steady transformation and there will remain many distractions and temptations all along the way.

Though you have chosen to leave your old nature

behind and become a new creation, it does not happen in one go. The 'desires of the flesh' do reappear.

But, remember, you are in a spiritual battle and you are on a journey. One day you will reach your destination and reside with Christ in Heavenly places.

Until then, you can choose to make steady progress, if this is what you desire.

**See how the lilies of the field grow.** *Matthew 6:28*

My child, do you not yet realise that you do not grow by struggling and striving – by rushing here and there – by attending every meeting and conference that there is available?

No…it is much easier – you grow by receiving – you receive by getting the balance correct between busyness and quietness.

In the quietness you become like Mary and sit at the feet of Jesus, listening. You don't even have to say anything. It does not need to be for long. You can also learn to do this when there is no time to sit still – in the midst of all the activity.

This is something you need to learn and then you will be clothed with the beauty and radiance of Jesus.

**Like clay in the hand of the potter, so are you in my hand.**
*Jeremiah 18:6b*

See the potter as he moulds the clay on his wheel. He begins with a shapeless form that is wet and slippery. He cups his hands around this, firmly and yet almost tenderly, holding the clay in place, to stop it from slithering and sliding about on the wheel where he has thrown it. Then he begins to re-shape and give life to the clay. Little by little he enables the clay to be fashioned, until the pot he desires has been created. If defects appear and it is not as he wishes it to be, he has the power to start again.

And so it is with you, My child, for I am the potter and you are the clay.

Yes, there are defects, but as you become willing to subject yourself to My breaking, melting, moulding and filling, so you too can become the person I have created you to be. All the impurities are removed and you become more like Christ in character, as I put in you His Nature.

You are so malleable in My Divine Hands, but I do need your co-operation to work within you and your willingness and desire to grow more like Christ.

Will you give Me permission to work?

**In all things God works for the good of those who love Him, who have been called according to His purpose.**
*Romans 8:28*

I am not saying that all that happens to you is good, for this is not so.

Many trials, storms, persecutions, sickness and accidents do come your way. Occasionally, I steer you clear of such things but not very often.

If unbelievers saw that you never succumbed to these things, there would be a rush to become believers – but for the wrong reasons.

No. You are a far greater witness to the world by revealing how you handle the unpleasant side of life. They will notice how you are able to remain at peace when all around you is raging. They will wonder at your calmness and serenity as you walk closely with Me. They will be amazed at your 'unruffled' state.

None of this is natural to humans – it has to be supernatural and from Me – wholly Divine.

So often in the testing times it will seem to you that there is no purpose – no fruit.

But always there will be a time of rejoicing when you have come through, for I will reveal to you the benefits – the personal, spiritual growth – the transformation – the refining when in the crucible – the deepening of our relationship.

**Be on your guard; stand firm in the faith; be men of courage.** *1 Corinthians 16:13*

You are free in Christ – free from the yoke of sin. Hold fast to the Truth and make sure you keep a firm grip on spiritual truths so that you do not fall into enemy territory and open the door to the powers of darkness.

Your strength must come always from the Lord Himself as His mighty Power works within you and for you.

Be watchful for the wiles and deceit of him who rules the world.

Be constant and fearless in witnessing and do not be intimidated by him.

Lean heavily on your God, trusting Me completely. Put your confidence in Me and in Me alone.

**Therefore, there is now no condemnation for those who are in Christ Jesus.** *Romans 8:1*

In the eyes of God the peoples of the world are condemned and without hope for their disobedience to My ways.

My Son was sent to change all of this. He died and rose again to make it possible for man to be reconciled to God once again, by the shedding of blood and the forgiveness of sins.

So many choose not to follow Him and go across the bridge to Me.

Christ is this bridge. Through Him you go free and are no longer guilty, because you have chosen this way.

All others who reject Christ and think that God will not turn them away are mistaken and My heart weeps for them, but I am unable to force My way into their lives – it is their decision.

## They will still bear fruit in old age, they will stay fresh and green. Psalm 92:14

If you believe in Me and trust Me wholeheartedly through the advancing years, you will remain strong spiritually, though your flesh may fail and your body become weak. This means that circumstances will not bend or break you.

If your faith is in Me there can still be a vitality and alertness, though you may not be able to run or even walk. None of the ills of old age can touch your spirit – only the flesh is weakened. You can grow in grace and be so rich in Love and contentment – rich in the verdure of trust in Me.

Even then, the eyes of those who look upon you will see your uprightness and your faithfulness. They will see the Christ in you, because you will shine and be radiant, due to your closeness to Me – what a witness! Such words of wisdom you will give to the younger ones. They will long to be with you and hold your hand, for they will 'feel' Christ, for such will be His Love and Peace in you – radiating from you. You can uplift them and challenge them to continue in the race – to persevere – encourage them to new heights of spiritual growth. You can continue to have new attitudes, a new perspective on life and a new frame of mind. You are rich in the experiences of life and there will be a serenity that can only come from years and years of walking with your God and developing a deep relationship with Him.

## Stand firm then, with the belt of truth buckled round your waist. *Ephesians 6:14*

There are so many things that would seek to distance you from the Truth of My Word.

Hold your ground and do not let anyone take it from you. Do not allow yourself to be robbed of all that is right and true. People can be very persuasive in trying to convince you that you are wrong in your beliefs and in your way of living. Satan is so subtle in the way that he seeks to control your mind and feed you with wrong thoughts. Another of his tactics is to distort My Truth and talk you into changing it slightly and so adapting it to suit yourself.

Just see for yourself how many times in the Gospels Christ says, "I tell you the truth,…".

Surely you desire the Truth and prefer it to lies.

I will guide you and teach you in My Truth by the power of the Holy Spirit.

I am the God of truth.

I ask you to love My Truth always and never 'water it down' in any way. What I say, I say and mean.

Live by My Truth at all times and be aware that lies can sometimes sound like the truth. Be discerning.

Ensure that your belt is buckled tightly around your waist. Never let it become loose or fall off.

**But store up for yourselves treasures in heaven...For where your treasure is, there your heart will be also.**
*Matthew 6:20-21*

What are these treasures – these riches – that I ask you to store up in Heaven?

They are all acts of obedience to Me as written in My Word.

So to store up these, you need to 'eat and digest' My Words thoroughly, for it is only then that you will know what they are.

Every little smile, every kindness, every gift to someone in need, every little seed you sow for My Kingdom, is adding to your Heavenly riches.

As you seek Me at the start of each day and indeed throughout the day, so you will be sowing for Me. Sometimes the treasures are big pearls of great price, sometimes tiny mustard seeds – they all count and are equal in My sight.

The more you fix your eyes on Me, the more you know My purposes for you, each day.

As you act in obedience to My will for you, so your treasure in Heaven grows and the more your desire will be to fulfil My commands. So, your heart, the core of your being, your very spirit, will want to seek this way of living.

### Abide in me, and I in you. *John 15:4 (KJV)*

Live in me, My child. Remain in Me at all times. Live in Me continually. I am the Bread of Life. Feed on My Word. Go on feeding on Me. Live continually in My forgiveness.

I tell you, My child, the one who feeds on Me and lives in My righteousness, will continue to live or abide in Me. And then, I will remain – continue – to live in him.

It is vital that you are obedient to this command, because only in this way will you be constantly aware of My presence with you and in you.

Only in this way can you walk daily, unafraid, because you can trust Me, knowing that I am 'in you' – part of you – all of you.

Only in this way of living do you have total power over the enemy and are equipped in every way necessary to overcome all trials and difficulties, hardship, persecutions, grief and opposition.

In order for Me to remain in you, you must live at one with Me and also at one with others. This involves being at peace with everyone. Pray for those who hurt you. Do not allow yourself to become disturbed and upset. Forgive immediately. Harbour no resentment, bitterness, anger or grudge.

I will give you rest and peace if you remain yoked with Me.

### Yet possessing every blessing, if our God our father be.
*Hymn*
Lead Us Heavenly Father Lead Us (James Edmeston Altd.)

Commit your life to Me; give every part of your being to Me. I am waiting, patiently knocking. Surrender absolutely all to Me, keeping nothing back.

In this way you will truly be able to say, 'Abba, Father.' You will be truly Mine and Mine alone.

Then you will discover all the rich inheritance that is there for you to take…the riches of the Heavenly places. I am yours and you are Mine. All that belongs to Me, belongs to you.

Take every thought captive for Me this day. Let Me be in all that you think, all that you do and all that you say. Then I can pour forth upon you all that I want to.

Do not look to man for rewards; they will come from Me, all unasked for, as you show your willingness to do My will and follow My Way.

## We are more than conquerors. *Romans 8:37*

Alone you are nothing and will be overcome easily and wounded by the ways of the world.

In Christ Jesus you are a conqueror always. You have been crucified with Christ and no longer live. It is Christ who lives in you and He always conquers. His victory is yours.

The sacrifice has been made for the sins of the world. The blood of Christ flowed at Calvary that you might have new life.

You are a new creation. The old has gone. Live out this new life of victory through Christ Jesus. See what Christ has done for you.

See all the riches and spiritual blessings that belong to you if only you will take them.

Stand firm on the promises of God, rebuke the evil one in the name of Jesus and be a conqueror with Him.

## With my God I can scale a wall. *Psalm 18:29b*

Nothing is impossible for God and nothing is impossible for you when you take His Hand in complete trust and walk according to His will and in

His Spirit.

You will soar as the eagle and with the strength that you think you lack. Your strength will come from God. He is the source of all you need and will gladly give to you. Listen to His voice and He will never ask you to do anything without giving you the grace by which it can be achieved.

Do not step out of line with Him. Do not let go of His Hand.

When you do this, you fail and things go wrong and tasks do become impossible.

Never try to plan your way. Always consult God. Always go His way and when you do stray, allow yourself to be led back willingly.

Then you will never cease to be surprised at what you can do.

### Give, and it will be given to you. Luke 6:38a

I would have you learn another way of Mine. In order that I meet all your needs, I ask of you one thing only and that is that you give.

Give of yourself. Give yourself to others and meet their needs, then I meet yours, even when you don't ask, always.

Give yourself – all of yourself – to Me that this law of Mine might be fulfilled.

There is so much that I want to give you.

Die to self completely and always, every day, be aware of what others require, be it practical, physical or spiritual.

Give, My child. Give always.

If you are uncertain what to give, ask Me and I will guide you.

You will find that I am a very generous giver and always give in great abundance – always – often much more than you need.

## God loves a cheerful giver. *2 Corinthians 9:7*

Give...give...give...that is My will for you. Be yourself and give of yourself.

There is but one rule that must apply...give cheerfully and not grudgingly...in no other way must you give. Remember, if there is any reluctance or resentment or unwillingness, then the giving is not of Me.

I live in you and it is Christ within you that you give to people.

As you do this, so you will receive from Me. Do not look to man for your rewards; they come from Me. I choose what to give you and when to give.

Give Me to everyone... My Love.

Give always without any seeking of personal gain.

Give of your time to others.

Giving is not always financial…you can give a smile or the touch of a hand to cheer someone on their way. Freely you receive so freely give.

That is My desire.

## For in Him we live and move and have our being.
*Acts 17:28*

You have accepted Me as Lord and Master of your life. You are under new ownership – that of God Himself. He has control of your life. Every event and circumstance is in His loving hands. Therefore, you do not have to depend on yourself.

Life is a glorious partnership between us. We do everything together. At no time will you be left alone. Everything you do, everything you think, everything you speak each moment of each day, we do together.

I am part of you. I am in you. No longer do you have to rely upon your own strength and resources. You have Mine to draw upon.

Live 'in Me' every day of your life.

Claim My promises to help you.

## But Christ lives in me. *Galatians 2:20*

When you gave your life to Me it was no longer yours but belonged to Me. As you became Mine, I, too, became yours.

Do you fully realise what this means?

All that I am, all that I have, I willingly share with you. What is Mine is yours too. My Strength is yours. My Energy is yours. My Love is yours. My Joy and Peace are yours.

Do you see?

You have all these things. I live in you, therefore these things are in you too.

So, when you feel worried, do not cling to the negative feeling…say, "I have the Peace of God," because this is true. This is what My Word says. Feed on the Word and believe it, not your feelings.

If you feel sad, say, "I have the oil of joy for mourning". Repeat this over and over again and as you do so, My Spirit will make it come true for you.

The positive Word of God will overcome your own negative feelings and the lies of the evil one. Cling fast to My Word and remember that you no longer live, but I, the Lord your God lives in you, reigns in you and should radiate from you at all times, in all you think, do and say, for others to see.

This is the way they will see and get to know Me too.

**Give, and it will be given to you.** *Luke 6:38*

What you give, my child, will determine what you receive.

It is so easy to judge and criticise, is it not?

Think of all I am willing to forgive in you.

Look upon yourself and be less quick to condemn others. Are there not mistakes in your life? Do you not get tired and weary and become irritable, sometimes saying things you do not mean, taking actions you wish you had not taken?

You come to Me in repentance and I always forgive you. I would like you to cultivate a forgiving spirit too and be less prone to reproach others...for that is My task, not yours.

A forgiving spirit demonstrates that you have received My forgiveness and wish to forgive others as I forgive you.

If I acted as you sometimes act, you would not like it. This is Love – the way of Love – My way.

If you are critical, you receive criticism. If you are generous in your giving to others – generous in time and talents, generous in love and compassion, generous in forgiving, these qualities will be returned to you in full measure from Me. I am a generous giver and give in abundance when I see My children obeying the Royal Law of Love and forgiveness.

# Part Ten

# Praise
and
Worship

**Give thanks to the Lord, for He is good; His love endures for ever.** *Psalm 107:1*

When you live in My Presence and stay close to Me daily, you will shine as stars in the Heavens above. This will be a good witness to others, of the God of Love.

For I am the One who saves all those in distress – those wanderers – those lost souls – those who walk in darkness. I am He. This is the extent of My Love. I break through into people's lives because I love them…because I want to.

So be thankful. Let thankfulness be constantly on your lips. Thank your God for His deliverance – for your salvation – and offer a sacrifice to Me of a faithful and obedient life.

**And forget not all His benefits.** *Psalm 103:2*

Things go wrong in your life…I know – they will – your earthly life will be troublesome.

When you are feeling low and burdened and overwhelmed, it is a good time to remember all My blessings and all that we have come through together. I know you will not feel like doing this; it has to be an act of the will and you need to be determined. It is always much easier to grumble and moan about life and dwell on all the things that are wrong.

All I give you, you receive without deserving any of it.

This is the extent of My Love for you – it is never ending.

When you feel you have nothing to praise Me for, read this psalm and then some of the others too. Write down all that there is to praise Me for. Life's journey is difficult – you are a pilgrim passing through. So make a written list of blessings from My Word and then add all your personal blessings, past and present.

Then you will see I am worthy of praise and that I love you dearly, especially in the tough times – they are character building.

## Give thanks in all circumstances. *I Thessalonians 5:18*

It is so easy to come to Me with thanksgiving in your heart and to enter My courts with praise for My Son, your Saviour, for His death and resurrection…for the abundant blessings which I love to shower upon those who walk in obedience and love to My commands.

But do you consider thanks for the times in your lives when you experience life-shattering problems – when your circumstances become seemingly impossible?

I do not send these to you but I do allow them to happen. Sometimes I turn them away and sometimes I don't do this. Sometimes, My purposes are brought about in your life only by seeing you in trials that shatter your peace. This is to remind you that everything in your life has Divine purpose – even the things that seem bad to you.

I do not expect you to thank me for such trials because I don't send them, but it is good to watch you accepting them and learning from them and through them.

In this way, you can thank Me for all that I teach you, when you are driven from the path of ease to seek My face.

## Always pray and (do) not give up. Luke 18:1

So many of My followers have had times of 'wrestling' with Me in prayer – Job, Jacob, Moses, Elijah – and of course, My Son Jesus Christ, when in the Garden of Gethsemane.

So do not be misled. There will be times in your life when you will find it very, very hard to pray. Others can join you then because prayer is teamwork also. But sometimes, it will be just you and Me and it will be hard work.

I ask you to persevere and not give up. Persist in prayer. Yes, you will have to struggle and grapple with Me. I have promised always to answer your prayers but there are times when it is right for you to wait – maybe for years. I urge you to keep on praying – to persevere – to be resolute – to stand your ground before Me and not turn away thinking I have not heard. I am listening always.

How much do you want My answer?

Have you thought deeply about what you are actually asking Me and what I might have to do, in order to give you your answer?

Is your prayer genuinely desired and according to My will?

Are your motives right?

Talk to Me about such things.

I am the giver of victory and prayer is victorious work. Remember the Lord is your banner.

**Praise the Lord, O my soul, and forget not all His benefits.**
*Psalm 103:2*

Fill every part of your being with praise for God.

This is what I ask you to desire – to seek – to want each day and each night of your life. For I am the Lord your God and am worthy of praise.

Praise is expressing to Me your appreciation and understanding of My worth. It is saying thank-you for each aspect of My Divine nature.

Do you realise that every time you praise Me you are helping yourself, by growing in awareness of who I am? Look at the psalms, for there you will find so many attributes – so many characteristics of your God for which you can thank Him.

Begin all your tasks by praising God; this can inspire

you to give of your best. Develop the practice of giving praise to God and you will experience greater joy and the strength to face anything.

I desire that you live with a praising heart and that praise and thanksgiving become a regular part of your daily routine – not just reserved only for celebrations.

Commit yourself to praise God daily. Praise the God who is your protector, your helper and your friend. Praise takes your mind off yourself, your problems and your circumstances and focuses on God.

Praise lifts your perspective from the earthly to the Heavenly.

Praise causes you to consider and appreciate My character – the Divine Nature itself.

### Praise the Lord, O my soul. *Psalm 146:1*

At all times, give Me thanks and praise.

Praise is the key that opens the door which allows My Love and blessings to flow to you.

There is such power in praise.

The evil one runs at the sound of people praising the mighty God.

Do not wait until you 'feel' like praising. Praise always, especially in the times of testing, when things are difficult. Praise is an act of the will and is not governed by feelings.

Praise is uplifting.

I delight in the voices of My children exalting Me and I inhabit the praises ascending from those who love Me and adore Me.

## He withdrew by boat privately to a solitary place.
Matthew 14:13

There is one thing that I ask of you. It is this…that you spend time alone with Me in prayer. Sometimes words will be spoken. Sometimes the prayer will be silent. You will do nothing but fix your eyes upon My face and gaze. As you do this, much of Me will be transferred to you. This is how you will become more like Me, which is My desire for you.

It is not always possible to be alone with Me in a quiet place, but I would have you always to begin each day this way. Let us spend time together at the dawn of each day, even if only for a few moments, talking and listening to each other.

This is the only way you can really get to know Me well and develop that personal relationship between us, which is what I want. This is the only way you will learn to recognise My voice instantly.

Spend much time listening; do not talk all the time. As you learn to do this, you will find it possible to 'draw apart' from the rush and bustle of the busy world and slip from it into the 'silence'. This is the secret of 'drawing apart' to be with Me. It can be done anywhere, any time of the day or night, even if there are crowds and noise around you. Just learn to take your eyes off all around you and gaze at Me. You will find yourself refreshed and strengthened every time, even if it is only a couple of minutes we spend together. Learn to spend a daily quiet time with Me and 'slip into the silence' throughout the day. I have so much to say to you...so much to teach you. Listen and you will hear My voice clearly.

**Give thanks in all circumstances.** *I Thessalonians 5:18*
Hymn: *Fill Thou My Life, O Lord My God* (Horatius Bonar)

> Fill every part of me with praise
> Let all my being speak
> Of Thee and of Thy love, O Lord,
> Poor though I be and weak.

Fellowship with Me every moment of the day and night. Let us never be apart from each other. That is My wish and My desire for us. Let us be as lovers, gazing into each other's faces, sometimes talking, sometimes listening, sometimes in silence, but always together and always aware of each other's presence.

Let us share our love for each other, but yet not keep it to ourselves. In your daily life, let My Love show and flow from Me, through you, to all others around.

It is something so wonderful, so deep, but to be shared in a world of lost, lonely, care-worn sheep.

Give My Love, My child. Live a life of love at all times. Give My Love. Keep your eyes ever open for ways of doing this, both great and small. So many, in fact everyone, needs love.

The Royal Law is Love; a command to love; firstly God and then your neighbour.

The rewards of this are great, abundant, bountiful and everlasting.

Never let your own circumstances and feelings stand in the way of this. I live in you. God is Love. Therefore Love lives in you and is always there to give.

Never deny anyone this Love. A heart full of Love, always has Love to give, remember.

Love conquers all, never fails and wins souls.

Because of this tremendous and powerful love, it is possible for you to give thanks in, not for, all circumstances. You know that whatever the situation, I am there in it with you and will see you through whatever happens.

**Let everything that has breath praise the Lord.** *Psalm 150:6*

Sing for joy, My daughter.

See the beauty of the world I have created for

you…the full moon, the silver pathway it makes across the restless sea; the thunder and the roar of the waves; the trees; the colours of autumn; the rain and hail; the rainbow with its many coloured hues; the birds and their flight; the blue of the sky and the fluffy white clouds; sunset and dawn; warmth, light, darkness – how majestic is My Name. Sing praises for creation and as you draw near to Me in this way and glorify My Name so I come close to you…helping, guiding, caring, loving, protecting, moulding, changing.

Rejoice and sing, for I am your God.

### Delight yourself in the Lord. *Psalm 37:4*

I delight in you and it is My desire that you will delight in Me.

I smile and am filled with overwhelming Love for you when you tell Me that you love Me. I long to hear these words and when I do, My Love just showers down upon you…not only upon you but into you also. Yes, it is true, that as you lift your hands in praise, worship and adoration, My Love overflows and drenches you. As your eyes turn Heavenwards and I see the love you have for Me in them, So My Love pours into you. This is how I inhabit the praises of My people.

The more you look to Me with words of praise, or even in silent adoration, the more I dwell in you.

Usually, you hear nothing and see nothing, though this is not always the case, but I ask you to receive from Me in faith...let Me minister to you...allow me to reach you deep inside.

I cannot help Myself when I watch your times of praise...I just have to reach down and bless you even more than you bless Me.

People will know and see and recognise the radiance and beauty of those who spend much time gazing upon My face in silent worship, because so much of Me will be in them.

## Praise Him for His grace and favour. *Hymn*
*Praise My Soul the King of Heaven* (Henry Frances Lyte)

Live a life of praise, My child...never for a moment forget who I am...what I am. Praise Me for this. I am Love...Love Divine. I am Peace...I am your Creator. These things deserve praise.

My Love is unmerited. My Favour is everlasting. I love you dearly. Honour Me with your praise...on the good days and yes, on the bad ones too. Praise is not determined by your feelings.

I am always the same...for ever and ever...the same each day of your life. My Love never wavers; it is constant. This surely makes Me worthy of your praise.

You may change, but can you see why it is important

to honour Me with your praise at all times?

I inhabit the praises of My people. As you lift your eyes to Me in praise, so you take them off yourself for a few moments.

Praise sent heavenwards is an important spiritual weapon – the evil one has to run.

## He...went away once more and prayed the third time, saying the same thing. *Matthew 26:44*

Prayer is communion with Me. I long to hear what you have to say to Me.

It is vital that you draw apart, even though our time together may be brief.

Do this each day.

Yes, sometimes it is important to be with others when you pray. But for just you and I to be alone together is so good too.

Do not worry about repeating the same thing. It is necessary to be persistent in prayer. Do not give up if the answer seems a long time coming. My timing is always right you know and sometimes I have to say no, for your own good. Never think for a moment that I don't hear your cries. This is not true, though I know you do sometimes wonder.

It is not always necessary to use words at all. I love the times when you sit at My feet and gaze at My face in silent love and adoration. I look upon you in a similar manner and minister to you in the way that is best at the time.

I long for you to love Me so much that your life becomes one of prayer; so that we are together all the time, doing everything together, conscious of each other's presence as we whisper silently to each other – not bearing to be apart.

### Give thanks in all circumstances. *I Thessalonians 5:18*

Sometimes you become weighed down by circumstances. You find it hard to pray, hard to be joyful and when you read that I expect you to give thanks, it feels as if you are unable to do this.

But you see I remain the same at all times and in all circumstances. I do not change and so you CAN give thanks for ME. You can bring praise and thanksgiving, NOT for the circumstances, but for ME, because I am in them with you and will remain with you, helping, guiding, sustaining, strengthening, and leading you through.

**Believe that you have received it, and it will be yours.**
*Mark 11:24b*

I look forward to the times you choose to draw close to Me. I long for you to turn to Me in prayer. These times of communion are cherished and I treasure them in My heart. I enjoy listening to all that you say and never think for a moment that I do not hear your words…I am never too busy and I do not take the phone off the hook as you sometimes imagine!

Three things I ask of you in your petitions though.

Firstly, come to Me with thanksgiving. Remember, do not be anxious about anything, but come in prayer and petition with thanksgiving, for I am a great God worthy to be praised and thanked, worshipped and adored.

Secondly, ask according to My will. This you will learn as you study and read the Scriptures because I am the author of these words. As you read you begin to understand My desires and My standards for living as one of My disciples.

Thirdly, I ask that you believe that you have received BEFORE you actually have. This is unusual for you I know, but it is what I ask. Just as a child trusts his earthly father to give an answer, so you must trust your Heavenly Father, knowing that I give only that which is part of My plan for you…a child lacks wisdom and does not always know what is best.

Part Eleven

# Serving God

**Faint not nor fear, His arms are near.** *Hymn*

*Fight the Good Fight* (John S.B.Monsell)

Have you ever gazed at a picture of the Good Shepherd cuddling a small lamb so tenderly in His arms? I ask you to put yourself in the place of that little lamb and look into My face.

Have you ever held a tiny baby in your arms and looked down upon their tiny face – perfect in every detail – so small – so very, very small and yet so trusting? Have you looked upon their eyes as they fix their gaze on your face? They know that your arms are cuddling them. They sense your love, your protection, your compassion, your tenderness, as you gently rock them and soothe them. They see gentleness in your eyes and such love and they feel safe and secure and wanted.

So it is for you, My child, if you can imagine yourself as that small lamb, that tiny babe, in My arms. There can be no fear or uncertainty in My arms – in My care – just trust Me. I love you dearly and long to cradle you in My arms to soothe you, as you nestle up to Me, especially in the long hours of the night or when your life is dark and you can no longer see the way ahead.

**Underneath are the everlasting arms.** *Deuteronomy 33:27*

Can you imagine what it is like to be a baby held in a father's or mother's arms?

Can you wonder why this often soothes a little one's cries and takes away their fears? It feels so safe. There is warmth, security and 'knowing' that all is well even if the pain does not go away. The little child will look into the eyes of the adult and see concern, love and compassion. They will feel protected and the trouble dwindles in their minds.

If a parent can do all this for their child, just by holding them tightly and closely to their heart, do you not realise that this is true when I hold My children in My arms? There is such love, such shelter from the storms of life in My arms. You are guarded; you are free from harm and danger, for I am dependable, reliable and trustworthy and you will find rest when I support you.

Think of an airbed floating on the water – it is impossible to sink it, isn't it?

That is how My arms are there under you. They are very strong and will never drop you – you are far too precious – far too treasured in My sight.

**Since we have been justified through faith, we have peace with God through our Lord Jesus Christ.** *Romans 5:1*

As My child you have been freed from the penalty of sin.

I look upon each child of Mine who is a repentant sinner through the blood of Christ and see that sinner as

Christ – that is, perfect.

I see each child as they can be and will be – growing in Christ and becoming more like Him day by day.

You can enjoy the Peace of being made right with God, but you will still face problems and difficulties each day. These are used by Me to help you to grow. So do not become discouraged. Instead, learn to depend on the power available to you as you live 'in Christ' – the power of the Holy Spirit and the Peace which will then rule in your hearts and guard your minds. For Peace floods the soul when Christ rules the heart.

### Delight yourself in the Lord. *Psalm 37:4*

In order to delight in Me, you will need to deepen your relationship with Me. This means spending more time with Me and getting to know Me through My Word and My actions in your life. Now I do not expect you to spend hours and hours on your knees alone with Me – this would not be possible. There is another way.

I wish you to learn how to practice the presence of God throughout your busy day in whatever you are doing. Commit everything to Me and so do it for Me. In this way your tasks are not so arduous. You can take pleasure in doing them for the Lord whom you love. You will be drawing close to Me as you do this and so I promise to draw close to you.

**On my bed I remember You; I think of You through the watches of the night. Because You are my help, I sing in the shadow of Your wings.** *Psalm 63:6-7*

I know just how many of you cannot sleep at night. There are various reasons for this – stress, worry and anxiety, illness, fear, depression, tension, lack of exercise – sleepless nights can be turned into times of great blessing however. Why not use them as quiet times with Me?

Ask for My help to turn your thoughts away from your problems and circumstances and on to Me. Ask for My help to quieten your racing thoughts. Put on the armour of God for protection. Then use the time to reflect on all that we have come through together, even though it has been a struggle for you much of the time. Count your blessings, name them one by one, as you recall just what the Lord has done.

Come to Me with a grateful, thankful heart and in praise. Use the silence and peace of the night to draw close to Me. If illness and pain trouble you ask for My Peace.

I know what you are going through and you will be safe in the arms of Jesus, whatever the outcome.

Rest, enfolded in My Love, though it may seem as though I do not care and am very silent when you need Me most.

As you try to do this and turn to Me, so I will help.

**But (He) made Himself nothing, taking the very nature of a servant.** *Philippians 2:7*

Christ is superior to angels, Moses and the high priests. He IS God – in a human body for a while. He is the exact representation of His being and yet He was willing to give up all His rights as the Son of God and, in obedience, come to live on earth to 'serve' people.

His attitude was that of a servant and as His followers, yours should be the same – to care for others – to look for their needs before your own – to serve out of love for God. So, each day, look for opportunities to serve others. They do not have to be huge tasks – the size of the deed makes no difference to Me.

Remember, you can choose your attitude.

**No-one who puts his hand to the plough and looks back is fit for service in the kingdom of God.** *Luke 9:62*

One more thing I ask from all those who choose to follow My path and that is total commitment. It is not possible to serve two masters and there can be no compromise.

You have to die with Jesus; to give up completely your old ways, habits and desires – your old way of living – and go My way. Your guide and helper is the Holy Spirit. He has been given to you to lead you into all truth.

I ask wholehearted dedication from you.

It is not right for you to pick and choose – to be obedient in some areas of your life and turn your back on other areas, ignoring My nudges and prompting to change. This will not really work and you are left in a very vulnerable position, opening up yourself to enemy attack. There is a cost to following Me and you must ask yourself if you are willing to pay the price of self-sacrifice.

It could mean that you do not always spend your time in the way that you would like to. It means giving your talents and gifts to Me to be used for My glory.

It is a different way of living and there will be countless distractions along the way.

**Let us please God by serving Him with thankful hearts.**
Hebrews 12:28 (TLB)

Without faith it is impossible to please God. But you have faith in a great God who saves. In giving your life to Christ you are part of His Kingdom – indeed, His Kingdom is within you.

One day, however, after a lot of shaking and sifting, the world will disappear and only My Kingdom will remain. You can be thankful because you are already part of this Kingdom and so you need have no fear for the future and the rapid approach of the end times.

No matter what happens, you will be able to stand firm with your feet placed firmly on the Rock.

My Kingdom is unshakeable – it is firm – it is stable – for this reason, offer to Me yourselves in service, gratefully, thankfully, with due reverence and awe.

### The God of peace. *Hebrews 13:20*

Jesus gives true Peace. Jesus is Peace. The Peace I give is completely contrary to that which the world calls peace.

My Peace is like the eye of the hurricane – quiet and calm while the storm rages around.

My Peace gives calmness and a serenity that cannot come from anywhere else or from anyone else.

It is not something that you can conjure up for yourselves. It is a quiet inner confidence in Me, that I am in control of all in your life and I will take care of you whatever happens.

The world's peace means no hassle of trouble – total tranquillity – quiet and stillness.

In a way this is what My Peace brings also, but it is different, in that you can have it when all around you is in total turmoil and anything but calm.

It is an inner knowing that all is well and will be well because I know what I'm doing – and I promise not to abandon you.

**You cannot serve both God and money.** Luke 16:13b

I know you need some money but beware, do not let it control your life, for it can then take the place of God and so become your master.

Some think there is power and control to be had in having a fortune.

Money cannot bring you good health or eternal life. It will never bring you great happiness as those in the world believe.

If your mind dwells much on money, how you can make more or what you can do with it, be warned – it is becoming your master instead of God!

Are you a generous, cheerful giver or do you hoard and save money for yourself?

Be wary of spending money you do not have and so find yourself getting into debt. Only spend what you can afford to spend.

All these things will show you to whom you look – who is your master?

Search your heart and see, for you cannot have two masters.

Is your security in money and possessions or is it in Christ and His Love and provision? The latter only will bring you Peace and joy.

**Great peace have they who love Your law.** *Psalm 119:165*

My Peace is obtained when you walk in the Spirit, in My strength and power, loving Me always and in obedience to My commands and to My Word.

There are great pressures upon you in your life on earth. I know. I have been there and it is not easy.

Only I can lift you above all this and it is then that you will know My Peace.

Seek Me – more of Me in you. Then you will be able to distinguish between what I am asking you to do and what man is expecting of you. Ask Me for discernment. I never overload you.

You will then have peace of mind.

**I have learned the secret of being content in any and every situation.** *Philippians 4:12*

My child, so often you lose My Peace and strive and struggle.

It is because you have momentarily forsaken Me and My Promises. You begin to move on your own and in your own strength. You step aside from My Power and My strength and everything becomes difficult. You grow weary and discouraged and lose heart.

"It's all too hard," you say.

With My help you can learn to change certain attitudes so that you accept My provision in all circumstances. Sometimes I do not change these, but I always keep My promise to provide your needs in them.

As you learn to trust Me, you too can soar on wings like the eagle – rising far above the situations that trouble you. There, you are above the mountains and as you look down you will see everything and everyone with My eyes and the mountains become much, much smaller. Fill the emptiness in your life with Me – not desires and wants.

I provide everything that I know is good for you because I am a loving Heavenly Father. Turn to Me as your source, especially for power and strength. Make sure your priorities are correct by seeking first My Kingdom. View every situation with My sight, thus making sure your focus is in the right place.

All this I will help you with if you but ask.

### Christ, in whom are hidden all the treasures of wisdom and knowledge. *Colossians 2:3*

I long for My children to grow nearer to each other in My Love. I long for them to find comfort and encouragement as they do this – that they may be strengthened. But even more, I long for each one of you to have intimacy with Christ Himself – that you deepen your relationship with Him and come to know Him better and more fully.

This, I desire, because He holds such treasures which

He keeps just for you. There are such riches and blessings in His hands that He waits to give you. He is keeper of a storehouse full of heavenly wealth and riches – there to be poured out upon you – such pearls of great price are in His possession and they are for you.

As you draw nearer to Him may you discover the ways and purposes of God and draw upon His wisdom and insight, so that you grow in spiritual knowledge.

Such treasures lie hidden in the hands of Him who loves you so much.

Seek Him and you will see just what He possesses for you.

## You guide me with Your counsel. *Psalm 73:24*

I am your leader and shepherd, who goes ahead of you always.

I know My sheep and, for each one, I have a unique plan and a unique path. As long as you stay close to Me and convince Me that you are really willing to go My way and fulfil My purposes in your life, I will not let you go astray for long.

Yes, you may take wrong turnings. You will make mistakes and there will be failures and disappointments, but let not these deter you or prevent you from getting up and going on again.

Persevere always, though the pathway be hard and

often mountainous. It may be that it is lonely too, but
do not give up. Tell Me about it. Seek Me, My wisdom
and guidance and you will find it.

Often My direction is not very clear and I know that
you struggle to discover exactly what I am saying.

All I ask is your willingness to follow and your
determination to continue.

My plans shall be fulfilled.

Request the wisdom and knowledge of other
believers, their prayer cover and spiritual direction also
and put your trust in Me for I shall keep My promises.

## With God all things are possible. *Matthew 19:26*

Is anything too hard or too wonderful for the Lord.
These were My words to Abraham.

Job knew that I could do all things.

I want you also to realise that I have plans and
purposes for each of My children and they will not be
prevented from being carried out. As long as you stay
close to Me and are willing to go hand in hand with Me
on your journey, they shall surely be fulfilled.

You may think you sometimes prevent My plans, by
going the wrong way – maybe delay, but not thwart
completely.

The impossible in your sight is easy for Me, so be
encouraged.

**Apart from me you can do nothing.** *John 15:5b*

I am the vine and you are the branches.

It is vital for each child of Mine to stay grafted to the vine and so rooted in Me. All the nourishment for your spiritual growth must come from Me and from Me alone. So often I see you planning your day, looking at your calendar and your diary and filling it so very full! You quickly become overloaded and the time spent with Me is cut shorter and shorter.

There will be many distractions each day. With the help of the Holy Spirit you must learn to sift and sort and keep your priorities right.

The moment you begin to step out on your own, in your own strength, you move away from Me. Your prayer time omits 'listening' time and you begin to say 'yes' to things that I have not asked you to do.

The evil one loves to keep you 'busy' for obvious reasons.

Your own efforts will not bear fruit and that is what I want from you.

**To man belong the plans of the heart, but from the Lord comes the reply of the tongue.** *Proverbs 16:1*

When I created you I gave you a mind and a brain. I intended that you should use these, both intellectually and creatively.

I desire you to plan your life and what you will do each day. However, this is always to be in co-operation with Me. The two of us are always to work together as one, walking hand in hand and taking each little step together – one step at a time.

Yes, you do need to seek the counsel of others also. But I want you to realise that the final outcome of each of your plans is in My Divine hands. I have a plan for you – that you will prosper and be successful. They are plans for your good – which will enable you to mature spiritually – that our relationship with each other will be deepened.

Sometimes you think your plans have all gone wrong because of this. It is not so.

The way I bring about My plan for your life does not always take the route that you would expect. My ways are not your ways and My thoughts are not your thoughts.

Ask for guidance as you plan and then move ahead in trust with each decision made.

I will not let you go astray if I see the desire and will in you to follow Me is genuine.

**Commit to the Lord whatever you do, and your plans will succeed.** *Proverbs 16:3*

It is very easy for you to think that you have been obedient to this command when you are really doing your task for yourself. You are working for your own advance – to boost your own ego or to gain a coveted position – and not for Me at all…or only in a half-hearted way.

Sometimes, when your plans seem to take an unexpected turn and move away from the route you thought they would take, you take charge and forget Me.

Trust Me and My judgement always and be ever mindful that I need to be part of your total plan.

Depend on Me and consult Me – not just at the onset, but all the way along the line.

Then, work hard, combining your effort with My provision.

Only in this way can there be success. I will ensure that your thoughts come in line with My will, when you do not push Me aside.

**Great peace have they who love Your law, and nothing can make them stumble.** *Psalm 119:165*

My Peace is unlike the peace of the world. It is a state of mind and heart that comes from trusting Me in all things and for all things.

It enables you to rise above the pressures, stresses and strains of daily living and remain calm and serene – standing tall – not falling – strong in the Lord and in His mighty Power. You will maintain an inward and outward tranquillity throughout your life, at every stage and every age. No-one will be able to remove it from you. Quietness and confident trust is the result of living according to My standards and forsaking all others.

My ways are honourable. I urge you to seek My righteousness that you too may be upright and God-fearing, for this alone is the way of Peace.

Seek first My Kingdom and My righteousness. This righteousness from God comes through faith – by believing with personal trust and by confident reliance in Jesus Christ, the Messiah. All are justified and made upright in My eyes, by My grace – by My unmerited favour and mercy – through the saving power of Christ.

Respond to My call and know that Christ is your Peace – only by living in Him will you possess this and so be strengthened and saved from falling.

**I will fear no evil, for You are with me.** *Psalm 23:4b*

Your only hope for total security is in Me – in My Love.

I am the only One who can accompany you on your journey through death. No-one else is able to do this. I alone am He who can lead you through to the other side.

When you find yourself in any dark valley – even when it does not lead to death – you feel as though you are in a bottomless pit, unable to climb out. It is like being in a deep, deep chasm – a void – a land as dark as midnight, where there is much confusion and not a glimmer of light. You may even wish that you had not been born.

But I am there with you. I am your shield – your only hope. I will lift your head at such times. Cry to Me for help.

Rest in My Love and stop struggling. A drowning man always thrashes about and so hinders his rescue. Be still. Trust in Me and in My Love. It never fails and will not let you go under. Stop striving. Stop even thinking.

Allow Me to fill you anew with My Love – to pour it all over you and enfold you with it.

Then you will know that no dark force can harm you. My perfect Love will eliminate all dread and fear.

### My purpose will stand, and I will do all that I please.
Isaiah 46:10b

I t is My purpose for you that surely stands firm and will come about as I have ordained.

Man proposes but it is God who disposes.

The Lord Almighty has purposed and no-one will

annul it. All that I pronounce will come to pass, for I do whatever I wish and it is for your good.

I am your God and I will make a way to bring about all that I desire for you.

You may seem to be in darkness, but I am the Light that shines in the darkness.

Whatever you attempt to pursue stay close to Me. Do nothing on your own.

Under My hand you will not cease to be fruitful.

## A person is justified by what he does and not by faith alone. *James 2:24*

It is not possible to live for Christ without living for others.

Each of My children is endowed with gifts from Me – to be used for others and to bring glory to Me. Whatever comes naturally to you can be put to great use for the benefit of others, if it is put into My Hands first. Look at your strengths – recognise them – give them to Me and see how, together, we can use them to reach others with My Love in some way.

Even a smiling face can really lift someone's spirit or a cheery 'Hello'. These may seem very insignificant to you, but are vitally important to the receiver and to Me, for you will have sown a seed that I can tend lovingly.

Never under-estimate each deed you do in Love.

All you do each day is really being done for Me anyway – or should be – the chores, the washing up.

Forsaking all, trust Me as we step out together, to reach others with the Love of God.

In this way you will be walking in obedience and so demonstrating that your faith is genuine – to walk in true faith will automatically result in deeds – it is putting your faith into action.

You are pronounced righteous before God through works of obedience as well as through what you believe…they are both important.

### We have this hope as an anchor for the soul, firm and secure. *Hebrews 6:19*

Such a hope I give to all My children.

There are two things about Me that will never cease to be – they are constant, reliable, and unchanging – you can depend upon them completely forever.

The first is My character – My Divine Nature.

The second is My Promises to you. I am a faithful God – a God of complete truth for whom it is impossible to lie.

You, by your faith, have put your trust in Me and just as an anchor from a ship is linked very strongly and firmly to that ship, so you have linked yourself to Me. An anchor that is buried deeply at the bottom of the ocean is immovable. The ship may drift slightly one way or the other but it cannot go far without the anchor being removed from the seabed.

You can choose whether you want to remain anchored to Me. It is a very safe and secure place…steadfast and sure…especially when the storm rages and the seas are mountainous.

Will you anchor yourself afresh?

Will you sink deeply into My Love?

**You heard my cry for mercy, when I called to You for help.**
*Psalm 31:22b*

M y help can come to you in many ways and often unexpected ways. So be alert and watch out when you have cried to Me for help.

Sometimes I send angels – in disguise – and you fail to recognise them and My answer.

When you are feeling low and discouraged and all around you seems dark and dreary, I may send a passer-by or someone in a shop, to make you laugh and remove the seriousness for a moment or two.

Take care how you treat strangers – they could be My ministering angels – they may come dressed very informally. Rarely will they be shining, dressed in white with large arched wings.

Occasionally you could find yourself in bed – even in

hospital – because I know you need a rest and also you will find time to listen to Me!

When you feel as though you have totally reached the end of the line, you cry out to me, "Why? Why?" Maybe, it is because I have a new direction for you and you should be wondering about the purpose I have behind whatever has befallen you.

Move beyond looking for explanations and ask Me what I am trying to teach you through the circumstances.

### Let us, therefore, make every effort to enter that rest.
Hebrews 4:11

As I have said so many times before, I ask you not to strive. You make your journey through life a lot harder than I intend it to be.

Do you realise what My Rest is and how much it will help you?

My Rest is My Peace. When you are at peace with yourself and also at peace with God, you are entering My Rest.

It requires effort on your part and a strong determination to accept My Promises as Truth. You can choose to accept your feelings, your thoughts or the lies of Satan. If you accept My Word and keep standing on it, by repeating it quietly to yourself many times a day or in the night, it will sink, lightly as a feather, from your mind into your heart – into your spirit – and become real to you.

When this happens you will be at peace, because you will be trusting Me to provide, to take control and to work.

So long as you persist in trying to work things out, you become increasingly weary and tense and you also limit how much I can do to help you.

So, all you need to strive to do is to be diligent in letting Me take over. When you don't know the next step, spend more time with Me, not less – just adoring Me – praising Me and worshipping Me trustfully – this brings My Peace.

## Serve wholeheartedly, as if you were serving the Lord, not men. *Ephesians 6:7*

Sometimes I watch you and you are so distressed and puzzled about serving Me because you don't see how you can do this. Your way seems to be blocked so often by men. You do not seem to be able to use your gifts as you think right.

Now, hear Me, for I am your God.

I never see tasks as big and important, or little and menial. This is not the way of the Lord. This is not what His eyes perceive. All that you do is important to Me – all that you accomplish each day as you 'plod' through your daily tasks and chores. All of this is service providing that you offer it to Me as such and by doing so, you are working for Me...not for yourself...not for anyone else...just for Me.

I know there are daily jobs which have to be done by you – scrubbing floors, going to work, preparing meals – shopping...I understand.

Do not see this as time wasted – time which is robbing you of 'special' service. You are serving Me in all of this if you tell Me you are doing it for Me and do it enthusiastically, being keen and zealous always.

## In Me you may have peace. *John 16:33*

When My Son left the earth on which you live and returned to be by My side, He did not leave you as orphans. You are not fatherless and never will be if you have committed your life to Christ, for you will always have a loving Heavenly Father who adores you.

But there is more.

If you belong to Christ and have chosen to follow Him and be His disciple, He will have come to live in you by His Spirit – the Holy Spirit.

He is your perfect everything – your teacher, your trainer, your comforter – the very voice and person of God inside you, united with your spirit. Thus, you are a son or daughter of God Himself. You have been given the greatest gift of all time and nothing and no-one can remove Him from you.

This gift brings peace of mind and heart.

The Peace I give is not fragile, flimsy and frail, like the peace which the world gives and which is so easily lost. No, indeed. My Peace brings great calmness and serenity which remains in the midst of trouble and persecution. So do not be afraid, anxious and worried about the future or the present.

"How long will I cope?" you say.

You won't, but I in you will and you can retain My Peace knowing this.

**Let him who walks in the dark, who has no light, trust in the name of the Lord and rely on his God.** Isaiah 50:10b

When your pathway is dark and you are completely unable to step ahead because you cannot see the way, just rest quietly in Me, in My Love and wait patiently and trustfully for My wisdom, My guidance and My leading.

Turn your thoughts to Me frequently and expectantly, for I am your strength and He who sustains.

You may not know what to do, but I see light always and My Light will lighten your darkness when the time is right. I will fulfil that which is My desire and purpose for you and it shall not be prevented or stopped. I shall be glorified through you.

Rest beneath the Almighty's shade, for I am your refuge and your sure defence. I will shield you from above, with the wings of My protection. You shall not be harmed.

Faith believes nor questions how or when. Faith asks not for understanding.

Mine is the triumph and the victory always. Do not be dismayed or discouraged, for you do not see what I see and you do not know what I know. I charge My angels to watch over you and guard your footsteps. When you are in the desert and the wasteland and when in hostile territory, you shall not be harmed, if you depend on Me completely and lay aside self. I will help you to believe in the darkness what you profess in the light.

**My peace I give you.** John 14:27

Take not the troubles of the world upon your shoulders. My back is strong and I am ready and willing to carry all your burdens and problems. Give them to Me and lighten your load.

Do not allow yourself to get so troubled by everyday events and circumstances. Remember that I am in full control of your life. Live in total surrender to Me at all times – moment by moment, every day.

Anything that bothers you, or any hurt that comes

your way, give to Me, My child. I say My child, because I love you and you are Mine.

Let My blessings flow through you and to you this day. I long for you to have so much, but cannot give unless you give to Me first.

Give yourself, all of yourself and you will know that inner peace of Mine that is strong enough to override all troublesome events, circumstances and hurts. It is yours. Take it today.

### Fix our eyes on Jesus. *Hebrews 12:2*

Let every day and every moment of your life be Christ-centred.

Whatever you do, do it for Me. Never fall into the trap of taking glory for yourself. Do not be proud and do not boast. My Spirit within you is gentle. Walk in quietness and confidence, trusting Me at all times in all you do, think and say. I am with you always and weep when I see you forgetting this and stepping into the ways of the world.

Be aware of evil at work to distract you and rebuke it quickly as I Myself did in the desert. You have armour to wear with which to quench every fiery dart that comes in your direction. Use it daily. Remember the victory has been won and the battle is Mine.

Let Me walk with you all the time. Feel My loving

Presence close to you, day and night. Talk to Me and listen. Keep your eyes on Me and all the things you need will be taken care of. Be conscious of doing My will…trust and obey, that is all I ask.

Never will you ever be alone. I will always protect you and lead you in My way if you are ready and willing to come. Though you stray, I will not allow you to go far. Though times are often dark I am there with you.

## Call upon me in the day of trouble. *Psalm 50:15*

I am always most attentive to the cries of each one of My children when they are in distress and not coping for one reason or another.

I will not hide My face from you whenever you need My help. I hear you when you cry. I answer you when you cry. I am the One who will deliver you and set you free from the snares of the evil one and from those who seek to harm you and cause you pain and hurt. I do not despise My captive people. I release you always and will not allow you to be engulfed by the floodwaters. The pit will not close its mouth over you. You will not be sucked under in the mire nor will you sink in the deep waters. The deep chasm will never swallow you up.

If you trust and obey Me, I will answer you when you call upon My Name in the day of disaster and in every trial and difficulty. I will have mercy on you, for I am a kind and forgiving God.

Give Me an undivided heart and walk always in My Truth.

Bring glory to Me. Praise My Name throughout the day and in the watches of the night also. Turn to Me and seek My face for I am a jealous God. Serve Me with gladness and come before Me with joyful praise. Exalt the Lord your God and worship Him for He is holy.

## When you pass through the waters, I will be with you.
Isaiah 43:2

Look expectantly for all your needs, especially when you are in deep water and cannot swim and your courage fails.

Know more of Christ, because in Him you will find all things and from Him you will receive all things. My supply is abundant and freely given.

I ask you to become God-dependent children and stop living as though you are self-sufficient.

This is My law of supply and demand and it is this and this alone that keeps the gate open and My help coming to you.

When trouble descends it is so easy to fall into panic, fear, anxiety and worry. The minute you do this, your eyes are on yourself and your problem and the gate begins to close. This is because you begin to focus on yourself and how you are going to cope and handle everything.

Look to Me instead. Keep your eyes on Me trustfully, expectantly waiting for Me to act – for this I shall surely do. I desire to lift you up and throw you a lifeline, but you will not catch it if you do not see it coming. Trust and do not doubt My promise to rescue you from all your foes. I know your feeble frame. My hands are here to bear you. My strength is never exhausted. My arms are everlasting.

Because I care about you so much, you can safely leave your cares with Me.

# Part Twelve

# Evangelism

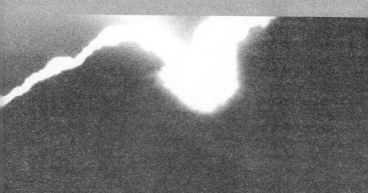

**Since my people are crushed, I am crushed; I mourn, and horror grips me.** *Jeremiah 8:21*

I weep.

I will tell you why; it is because I see that My children who know Me and love Me are often so unwilling to make this Love known to unbelievers.

I weep and weep, for you are My Hands; you are My Tongue; you are My Love and these people, hundreds and hundreds of them, are lost.

Does it not grip you with horror too, as it did Jeremiah, to see people reject God? Is there no emotion in you as in him, when you see so many in the world dying in sin? Does it not fill you with anguish also?

Why are your hearts not breaking for these people… your neighbours, your friends, the young ones, oh, the bewildered young ones, your family?

How I long for you to ask Me to give you a passion for the lost, so that you will be moved to help.

When, oh, when, will you ask God, your God, to break your hearts for the world He loves?

I implore you to do this and then plead with Me to save these people.

Don't give up because they don't seem to change. Meet them where they are.

Get on your knees and weep for their salvation.

**Let your light shine before men, that they may see your good deeds and praise your Father in heaven.** *Matthew 5:16*

Whatever your circumstances are, there is always someone, somewhere who needs a helping hand or even just a smile.

Never let a day pass without serving Me in some way. Do not be misled by thinking that the deeds must be great…little things mean a lot. Serve Me in small ways. I will then give you greater tasks to do. Just be yourself. Keep your eyes and ears open for someone who needs cheering. Listen to My voice. I will tell you where to go and what to do.

In this way, people will see My Kindness and My Love, My Compassion and Gentleness, shining forth from you. Be a candle in the darkness around you.

Before long, other candles will be alight and there will be much rejoicing in Heaven as you lead people to Me, but in a very unobtrusive way.

Watch and see My Power at work as you serve, both in yourself and in the lives of those around you.

**Store up for yourselves treasures in heaven.** *Matthew 6:20*

All that win souls are wise, for those who have helped to lead others to Christ will find the fullest of Heaven's joys.

Christ commands you too to, "Go tell". There are

many ways of doing this.

The most simple is by the way that you live your ordinary, everyday, run-of-the-mill life.

You never know who is watching you and your reactions and words. The more time you spend in My Presence, the more I will abide in you and the more you will reflect My image – the more people will see the Christ in you and recognise that somehow you are different.

Your life is busy, purposeful and there are many demands – or you may be an invalid, or housebound – you may be on a sick-bed – this makes no difference.

I would ask you to learn how to practise living in the presence of God all day. I would ask you to learn how to live a life of prayer – in the busyness and rush – in the sleepless nights and lonely days – in the darkness and in the storms – in the light and in days of joy. Soak Me up – soak up My Love and My characteristics, as blotting paper soaks up ink. Let all of Me spread everywhere, to touch the lives of many in various ways each day.

Lay up 'pleasures' for yourself in Heaven, as you look forward to meeting all those who have followed your example by what they have seen in you.

## Go, go into the world. *Chorus*

Extract taken from the song: *I Give You Now All I Have Go!* (Amy Rose) ©1988 Coronation Music Publishing/Kingsway's Thankyou Music, P.O. Box 75, Eastbourne, East Sussex, BN23 6NW, UK. For the UK, Australia & New Zealand. Used by permission.

Keep plugged in to your source! Power only flows through when contact is made. When you are re-charged then 'GO', in My Divine Name, to carry Me and My Divine Love to the lost, the lonely, the bewildered and confused.

Do not store up all that I give you for yourself. Be always ready and alert to give out what I give to you. All that I pour into you, I wish you to release to others. Move out and launch into the deep with acts of faith – for without faith it is impossible to please God.

I charge your battery that you may release its energy to the needy. I commission you to 'GO'.

## Acknowledgements

I would like to thank you Angus, for all your hard work and the time you have given to help me prepare this book for publication...also for your wise counsel and wisdom in the paper work and using the computer. You just took over the running of the household for me. Without you I could not have done it.

I would like to thank the three vicars who were there when my need was so great and for the guidance, comfort and encouragement they gave to me when all was very dark...Rev. Martin Greig, Rev. Peter Pullin and Rev. Peter Beresford.

Thank you Keith, for providing a much needed listening ear so many times.

Thank you Lin, as well, for encouraging me to go ahead and make these words available to others.

Thank you Anne O'Rorke, for sorting out the meditations and for being so patient and also the other staff involved at John Hunt Publishing, not forgetting John himself who accepted the work.

Lastly I would remember with such love, my parents and grandmothers who started me off on the right road...the way of Jesus Christ, my Lord and Saviour.

**TO HIM BE THE GLORY FOR EVER AND EVER.**